Theory
of
Film Practice

NOËL BURCH

TRANSLATED BY HELEN R. LANE

PRINCETON UNIVERSITY PRESS
PRINCETON, NEW JERSEY

Contents

iii

Foreword

"I" am not the author of this book.

The name on the cover is the same, but the "I" writing this foreword is in so many ways not the "I" who wrote the book fourteen years ago that he feels compelled to dissociate the two.

That other "I" was an American expatriate of thirty-five who, fifteen years earlier, had decided to make his home in Paris, largely because of a fascination with what he knew of French film culture (he had seen *le Diable au Corps* some fifteen times), who had attended the French national film school (IDHEC), who had tried to the best of his ability to carve a niche for himself in the industry and who had failed . . . mainly because he was subjectively unequipped to cope with the values, the mores, the personalities of show business, however "cultural" its veneer in Paris.

This book, then, was a fantasy-creation, a set of prescriptions for film-making, laid down by someone who had (almost) never made a film. *It stood in lieu of those unmade films.*

This book also determined a somewhat misbegotten vocation: teaching, writing, "theorizing," translations into half a dozen languages, two more books, an International Reputation . . . very little film-making, however, with the exception of a number of television programs, and eventually the (temporary) abandonment of hope in that direction. Paradoxically, however, the reputation as a theoretician seems to have made film-making possible again, for which the present "I" is extremely grateful since, when all is said and done, that is what he does best.

For several years now, this book has been a great source of embarrassment to me. So too, in many ways, has my career as a "theoretician," largely founded on insight and speculation, rather than on any sound grasp of modern theoretical disciplines. I have had no university education to speak of and have never really done the homework that might have made up for this lack. Consequently, for ten years at least, I have been *standing on tiptoes*, which can grow to be very tiring.

Yet it has also been brought home to me, often enough, that this book in particular has been found extremely useful by some educators, extremely stimulating by some film-makers.

It is impossible for me simply to dismiss such "testimonials," which presumably justify the present reprint.

The source of embarrassment here is simple enough to name: formalism. A formalism of the worst kind, which might also be called "musicalism" or, perhaps most precisely, *flight from meaning*. The book is shot through with a paradox: on the one hand, a neurotic rejection of "content" (a rejection which, autobiographically, may be seen to have stemmed from a studied ignorance and *fear* of the political), and, on the other, an equally neurotic insistence on finding abstract, quasi-musical values in . . . mainstream cinema. For indeed, at the time of writing, I was almost wholly unfamiliar with the New American Cinema (some of the most important productions of which, I might add, were yet to come) and felt sympathetic towards only some of the more tradition-related aspects of it. Today, although my familiarity with that cinema is greater, and I recognize the considerable importance of a movement now apparently deceased, I am not at all sure today that this was the book's most serious blind spot.

The "I" of the 1960s had a "vision" of cinema and was impatient with what appeared to be just about everyone else's blindness to the Truth: that, for example, the films of Eisenstein, Resnais, Antonioni, Bergman and others—a certain, rather ingenuous, eclecticism was, perhaps, a virtue here—"stood out above the pack" not because of the stories they told—everybody told stories, and theirs were not fundamentally different—but because of Something Else, because of the way in which they organized the formal parameters of their discourse. Today, having learned a few concepts from semiology, though I am no semiotician and wish that even less informed authors would stop saying that I am—I would identify this difference as having to do with *the work of the signifier*.

These films, then, "stood out above the pack." . . . Here, of course, is the other glaring blind spot in my thinking at that time: an unabashed elitism. Unconcerned as I was with the material and mental life of society as a whole, I was equally unconcerned with the films that it saw, with the ways in which it saw or was made to see them. Now that these are almost my only concern, I have difficulty in looking back with much sympathy on a writer obsessed with singling out from among the vast corpus of world film production only those small areas of cultural respectability wherein film rose to the heights of Great Art—a writer for whom the "purity" of classical music was an intangible, absolute model.

Actually, of course, this was not a critical or a theoretical stance at all. I was simply describing—and illustrating—a methodology which I wished to use in my own work, and which at that time involved only an extension of the classical narrative system rather than a rejection or "deconstruction" of it, as I have since at times envisioned for myself, advocated for others. I had already applied this methodology in bits and pieces—the unfinished *le Bleu du Ciel*, *Noviciat*, my contributions to *Cinéastes de Notre Temps* and I would say that even today, in planning or making films, I still tend to call upon its tenets. This is what is "left" of the book for me.

And it is not that I think, today, that the approach to be found in these pages was "wrong," that the descriptions and analyses set forth here are purely fantasmatic. What I "saw" in these films, with perhaps a few minor exceptions, "is there." But this approach was singularly narrow and incomplete, leading, for example, to the contemplation of a master such as Hitchcock, of whom I had no real understanding, through the wrong end of the telescope. Had I bothered to re-view such an incomparable masterpiece as *Shadow of a Doubt*, it is unlikely that I would have even understood its complexities.

What was lacking were the concepts of textuality, of polysemia, of the multiplicity and ambivalence of film-work, of cinema as institution. I wanted narrative film to have what I saw as the "purity" of opera. But of course that purity was just one more fantasy, woven by someone who was content to listen to or even watch opera with only the haziest knowledge of the libretto, who read Mallarmé and *Finnegan's Wake* aloud "for the sound."

Today, I am sorry to observe that this formalist approach to cinema—albeit in slightly more sophisticated guises—has gained considerable following in the country of my birth, where the political culture which has forestalled such foolishness in Italy, France and even England, is sadly lacking. And although it would be excessively masochistic of me to take all the blame for this state of affairs— which is due also to the extreme compartmentalization of this country's intellectual and artistic community—it is clear to me that I have a not inconsiderable share of it to live down.

And yet in spite of all this, the practical virtues of such an approach in my work and others'—especially as regards the initiation of young people whose film experience is limited to institutional productions—appear to be real enough. To the mass of filmgoers, after all, what is *in focus* is, indeed, the diegesis, the illusory "world-experience" of film. The work of the signifier, however sophisticated, so long as it "keeps a low profile," so long as it does not draw a curtain of semantic noise between that "world beyond the screen" and the "average spectator," is invariably so "out of focus" as to be indeed quite invisible. Thus, to the extent that this book, especially in its first two sections, does operate a sort of "focus-pull," encouraging the reader/viewer to look at what camera, editing, etc. are doing *too*, it has had, I take it, a corrosive, salutary effect in many instances.

But I do suggest that readers take with a large spoonful of salt many of the value judgements expressed herein. I certainly do not feel that the films of Alain Resnais, let alone those of Alain Robbe-

Grillet, are very useful models for today. The fact that the "I" of this book saw them as such is only one more indication of a youthful attachment to the concept of "art for art's sake" which provided an expatriate American, ideologically and politically rootless, with a way of shutting out the tensions and conflicts of a European society where class struggle had (has) a totally different status from that which it had (has) in the society in which he had been raised.

The reader must also be wary of attempts found here to inscribe cinematic stylistics into some sort of mathesis. Although I regard the first chapter of this book as in many ways the most seminal of all, the rather solemn pronouncement that there are fifteen types of spatio-temporal shot-association is assuredly one of the most useless pieces of information about film-making that has ever been set forth in print.

On the other hand, it is true that the aspiration towards a stylistics involving a "dialectical extension" of the traditional system of *découpage* (already partially advocated by Eisenstein although I was unaware of this at the time) has since found objective echo in the work of certain modern masters (Oshima's *The Hanging* and *Floating Ghosts at Noon*, the opening sequences of Antonioni's *The Passenger* or Visconti's *Ludwig*). And the work of at least one young maker—Paolino Viota's *Contactos*, which I am not embarrassed to say that I admire immensely—was openly influenced by certain pages of this book. However, it would be a patent trivialization to *reduce* any of these films to such formal concerns (*Contactos* is an admirable tribute to the resistance under Franco), just as it was to reduce Renoir's *Nana* to a "structure" of the exploitation of off-screen space, or *Cronaca di un Amore* to a visual "ballet" between camera and actors.

Clearly—and I have made no bones of it over the last five or six years—I have come to have a low opinion of this book, at least as "theory." The chapter entitled "Structures of Agression" is mostly arrant nonsense, while the final pair, although they do contain a plea for a breakdown of the traditional barriers between "fiction" and "documentary" which is still central to my work as a filmmaker are, from a theoretical point of view, quite untenable, as nearly every European critic worthy of the name was quick to point out.

The French term for foreword is *avertissement*. I hope that readers will find that to be forewarned is both to avoid muttered polemics with a dead boy who grew up to regret the error of his ways and to sift out the nuggets that may still lie among the dross he mined.

Venice, September 1980

1

Basic Elements

1

Spatial and Temporal Articulations

The terminology a film-maker or film theoretician chooses to employ is a significant reflection of what he takes a film to be. The French term *découpage technique* or simply *découpage*[1] with its several related meanings is a case in point. In everyday practice, *découpage* refers to the final form of a script, incorporating whatever technical information the director feels it necessary to set down on paper to enable a production crew to understand his intention and find the technical means with which to fulfill it, to help them plan their work in terms of his. By extension, but still on the same practical workaday level, *découpage* also refers to the more or less precise breakdown of a narrative action into separate shots and sequences *before filming*. French film-makers, of course, are not the only ones to have a term for this procedure. Both English- and Italian-speaking film-makers have a similar term for this final version of the script—called a "shooting script" in English and a *copione* in Italian—though they always speak of "writing" it or "establishing" it, thereby indicating that the operation the word describes is no more important in their minds than any other in the making of a film. A third French meaning of *découpage*, however, has no English equivalent. Although obviously derived from the second meaning of a shot

3

breakdown, it is quite distinct from it, no longer referring to a process taking place before filming or to a particular technical operation but, rather, to the underlying structure of the *finished* film. Formally, a film consists of a succession of fragments excerpted from a spatial and temporal continuum. *Découpage* in its third French meaning refers to what results when the spatial fragments, or, more accurately, the succession of spatial fragments excerpted in the shooting process, converge with the temporal fragments whose duration may be roughly determined during the shooting, but whose final duration is established only on the editing table. The dialectical notion inherent in the term *découpage* enables us to determine, and therefore to analyze, the specific form of a film, its essential unfolding in time and space. *Découpage* as a structural concept involving a synthesis is strictly a French notion. An American film-maker (or film critic, in so far as American film critics are interested in film technique at all) conceives of a film as involving two successive and separate operations, the selection of a camera setup and then the cutting of the filmed images. It may never occur to English-speaking film-makers or English-speaking critics that these two operations stem from a single underlying concept, simply because they have at their disposal no single word for this concept. If many of the most important formal break-throughs in film in the last fifteen years[2] have occurred in France, it may be in part a matter of vocabulary.

An examination of the actual manner in which the two partial *découpages*, one temporal and the other spatial, join together to create a single articulated formal texture enables us to classify the possible ways of joining together the spaces depicted by two succeeding camera setups and the different ways of joining together two temporal situations. Such classification of the possible forms of temporal and spatial articulations between two shots might seem to be a rather academic endeavor, but to my knowledge no one has previously attempted such a classification, and I believe that it may well open up some important new perspectives.

Setting aside such "punctuation marks" as dissolves and wipes, which may be regarded as mere variations on the straight cut, five distinct types of temporal articulation between any two shots are possible.

The two shots, first of all, may be absolutely continuous. In a certain sense, the clearest example of this sort of temporal continuity is a cut from a shot of someone speaking to a shot of someone listening, with the dialogue continuing without a break in voice-over. This is, of course, precisely what happens whenever a shot is followed by a reverse-angle shot. Although the term "straight match-cut," as is made clear later on in this chapter, refers more specifically to spatial continuity, it is also another example of absolute temporal continuity. If shot A shows someone coming up to a door, putting his hand on the doorknob, turning it, then starting to open the door, shot B, perhaps taken from the other side of the door, can pick up the action at the precise point where the previous shot left off and show the rest of the action as it would have "actually" occurred, with the person coming through the door and so on. This action could even conceivably be filmed by two cameras simultaneously, resulting in two shots[3] that, taken together, preserve an absolute continuity of action seen from two different angles. To obtain as complete a continuity in the edited film, all we would have to do is cut the tail of shot A into the head of shot B on the editing table.

A second possible type of temporal relationship between two shots involves the presence of a gap between them, constituting what might be called a *temporal ellipsis* or *time abridgement*. Referring again to the example of someone opening a door filmed by two cameras (or by the same camera from two different angles), a part of the action might be omitted when these two shots are joined together (in shot A someone puts his hand on the doorknob and turns it; in shot B he closes the door behind him). Even the most conventional films frequently use this technique as a means of tightening the action, of eliminating the superfluous. In shot A someone might perhaps start up a flight of stairs, and in shot B he might already be on the second or even the fifth floor. Particularly when a simple action such as opening a door and walking through it is involved, it might be emphasized that the ellipsis or abridgement can occur in any one of a large number of possible variations; the "real" action might span some five or six seconds, and the time ellipsis might involve the omission of anything from a twenty-fourth of a second to several seconds, and might occur at any point in the action. This is equally true in the case of absolute temporal continuity; the transition between shots may occur anywhere. A film editor might maintain that in both cases there is only one "right" point at which to make a straight match-cut or abridge the action, but what he really means is that there is only one place where the shot transition will not be consciously noticed by the viewer.[4] This may well be. But if we are seeking a film style that is less "smooth," that actually stresses the structures that it is based upon, a whole range of possibilities remains open.

This first type of temporal ellipsis involves, then, an omission of a time-span that is not only perceptible but *measurable* as well. The occurrence and the extent of the omission are necessarily always indicated by a more or less noticeable break in either a visual or an auditory action that is potentially capable of being completely continuous. (A continuous temporal-auditory action, verbal or otherwise, occurring in conjunction with a discontinuous temporal-visual action, as in Jean-Luc Godard's *Breathless* and Louis Malle's *Zazie dans le Métro*, is, of course, not at all precluded.) In the previous examples of going through a door or going up a flight of stairs we become aware of the existence of a temporal discontinuity or gap as a result of the spatial continuity having been forcefully enough maintained to allow the viewer to determine mentally that some portion of a continuous action has been omitted and even enable him to "measure" the actual extent of the omission. (Temporal *continuity* can likewise only be measured relative to some other *uninterrupted* visual or auditory continuity.) Thus, if a shot transition takes us from one location to another, more distant one without there being any way of relating the two distinct spaces (such as a telephone or some other means of communication), the temporal continuity between them will remain indefinite unless it is preserved through the use of such clumsy devices as successive close-ups of a clock-dial or some convention such as cross-cutting, an emphatic alternation between two actions occurring in two distinct spaces.[5]

A third type of temporal articulation and a second type of abridgement are possible, the "*indefinite ellipsis.*" It may cover an hour or a year, the exact extent of the temporal omission being measurable only through the aid of something "external"—a line of dialogue, a title, a clock, a calendar, a change in dress style, or the like. It is closely related to the scenario, to the actual narrative and visual content, but it nonetheless performs a genuine temporal function,[6] for, even though the time of the narrative obviously is not the same as the time of the film, the two time spans can nevertheless be related in a rigorously dialectical manner. The reader may object that the boundary between the "measurable" ellipsis and the "indefinite" ellipsis is not clear. Admittedly a segment of time abridged in the process of splicing together two shots showing someone walking through a door can be measured rather accurately—namely, as that part of the action that we know must be gone through but do not see, whereas we are less capable of measuring "the time it takes to climb five flights of stairs." However, "the time it takes to climb five flights of stairs" still constitutes a unit of measurement, much as "one candle power" is the amount of light furnished by one candle; this is not at all the case, on the other hand, when we realize that something is occurring "a few days later," as in an indefinite ellipsis.

A *time reversal* constitutes another type of possible temporal articulation. In the example of someone walking through a door, shot A might have included the entire action up to the moment of going through the door, with shot B going back to the moment when the door was opened, repeating part of the action in a deliberately artificial manner. This procedure constitutes what might be called a *short time reversal*, or an overlapping cut, such as Sergei Eisenstein used so often and to such striking advantage—as in the bridge sequence in *October* (*Ten Days That Shook the World*)—and such as certain avant-garde film-makers have used (see also François Truffaut's *La Peau douce* and Luis Buñuel's *The Exterminating Angel*. At this point, however, it is worth noting that time reversals, like time ellipses, are commonly used on a very small scale, involving the omission or repetition of only a few frames, as a means of preserving *apparent* continuity. The preservation of an appearance of continuity is, of course, what is always involved in any conventional use of time abridgement. What we are referring to now, however, no longer involves simple mental deception—that is to say, making an action that is not visually continuous convey a "spirit" of continuity—but the actual physical deception of the eye. When it comes to "match-cutting" two shots showing someone walking through a door, for perceptual reasons which are quite beyond the scope of this book), a few frames of the action may be omitted or repeated in order that the filmed action may seem more smoothly continuous than would have been the case had the shot been picked up *precisely* where the previous one left off.

The flashback is a more usual form of time reversal. Just as a time ellipsis can span either just a few seconds or several years, so too can a time reversal. The fifth and last type of temporal articulation thus is the *indefinite time reversal*, which is analogous to the *indefinite time ellipsis* (the exact extent of a flashback is as difficult to measure without outside clues as is the extent of a flashforward) and the opposite of a *measurable time reversal*. The reason why the flashback so often seems such a dated and essentially uncinematic technique today is that, aside from its use by Alain Resnais and in a few isolated films such as Marcel Carné's *Le Jour se lève* and Marcel Hanoun's *Une Simple histoire*, the formal function of the flashback and its precise relationship to other forms of temporal articulation have never been understood. Like the voice-over, the flashback has remained little more than a convenient narrative device borrowed from the novel, although both have recently begun to assume other functions.

But might not this inability to measure the exact temporal duration spanned by either flashback or flashforward point to some basic and previously overlooked truth? Are not jumps forward and backward in time really identical on the formal organic level of a film? Are there not ultimately, then, only four kinds of temporal relationships, the fourth consisting of a great jump in time, either forward or backward? Alain Robbe-Grillet obviously believes this is so, and in that sense, his and Resnais's *Last Year at Marienbad* perhaps comes closer to the organic essence of film than it is currently fashionable to believe.

*   *   *

Three types of articulation between the spaces depicted in two successive shots are possible—apart from, and independent of, temporal articulations, even though they have obvious analogies to them.

A first kind of possible spatial relationship between two shots involves the preservation of spatial continuity in a manner similar to that in which temporal continuity is preserved, *although this spatial continuity may or may not be accompanied by temporal continuity.*

The door example in all three variations is an instance of spatial continuity; in each case, the same fragment of space fully or partially seen in shot A is also visible in shot B. Any change in angle or scale (matching shots, that is, taken from the same angle but closer or farther away) with relation to the same camera subject or within the same location or the same circumscribed space generally establishes a spatial continuity between two shots. That much is obvious. It seems to follow that there is only one other form of possible spatial articulation between two shots: spatial *discontinuity*—in other words, anything not falling into the first category. This discontinuity, however, can be divided into two distinct subtypes bearing a rather curious resemblance to the two distinct subtypes of time ellipses and reversals. While showing a space different in every way from the space visible in shot A, shot B can show a space that is obviously in close *proximity* to the spatial fragment previously seen (it may, for instance, be within the same room or other closed or circumscribed space). This type of spatial discontinuity has given rise to a whole vocabulary dealing with spatial orientation, and the fact that such a vocabulary should be necessary serves to emphasize how essentially different this type is from an obvious third possibility, complete and radical spatial discontinuity.

This vocabulary dealing with spatial orientation brings us to a key term, one of some concern to us here: the "match" or "match-cut." "Match" refers to any element having to do with the preservation of continuity between two or more shots. Props, for instance, can be "match" or "not match." On a sound stage one can often hear remarks such as "these glasses are not match," meaning that the actor was not wearing the same glasses or was not wearing glasses at all in a shot that has already been filmed and is supposed to "match" with the shot at hand. "Match" can also refer to space, as in eye-line matches, matches in screen direction, and matches in the position of people or objects on screen. There are also spatiotemporal matches, as in the door example, where the speed of movement in the two shots must "match," that is, must *appear* to be the same. To clarify this notion of "match" or "match-cutting," a brief history of how it developed is in order.

When, between 1905 and 1920, film-makers started bringing their cameras up close to the actors and *fragmenting* the "proscenium

space" that early cinema had left intact, they noticed that, if they
wanted to maintain the illusion of theatrical space, a "real" space
in which the viewer has an immediate and constant sense of orientation (and this was, and still remains, the essential aim for many
directors), certain rules had to be respected if the viewer was not
to lose his footing, to lose that instinctive sense of direction he
always has in traditional theater and believes he has in life. This
was the source of the concepts of eye-line match, matching screen
direction, and matching screen position.

Eye-line match and matching screen direction concern two shots
that are spatially discontinuous but in close proximity. When two
shots show two different persons supposedly looking at each other,
person A must look screen right and person B screen left, or vice versa,
for if both look in the same direction in two successive shots, the
viewer will inevitably have the impression that they are not looking
at each other and will suddenly feel that he has completely lost his
orientation in screen space. This observation on the part of the second generation of film-makers contains a basic truth that goes far
beyond the original goal of matching. Only the Russian directors,
however (before Stalinism brought film experimentation to an
abrupt halt), were beginning to glimpse what this really implied:
that only what happens in frame is important, that the only film
space is screen space, that screen space can be manipulated through
the use of an infinite variety of *possible* real spaces, and that dis-
orienting the viewer is one of a film-maker's most valuable tools. We
will come back to this idea later.

As a corollary to eye-line match, film-makers also discovered the
principle of matching screen direction: Someone or something exiting frame left must always enter a new frame showing a space that
is supposedly close by or contiguous from the right; if this does not
occur it will seem that there has been a change in the direction the
person or object is moving in.

It was also noticed, finally, that in any situation involving two
shots preserving spatial continuity and showing two people seen
from relatively close up, their respective screen positions as established in the first shot, with one of them perhaps to the right and the
other to the left, must not be changed in succeeding shots. To do so
risks confusing the viewer's eye, for he invariably will read any

shift in screen position as necessarily corresponding to a shift in "real" space.

As the techniques for breaking down an action into shots and sequences were developed and refined, these continuity rules became more and more firmly fixed,[7] methods ensuring that they would be respected were perfected,[8] and their underlying aim, to make any transition between two shots that were spatially continuous or in close proximity *imperceptible*, became increasingly apparent. The introduction of sound brought an increased emphasis on film as an essentially "realistic" medium, an erroneous conception that soon resulted in what we might call the "zero point of cinematic style," at least in so far as shot transitions were concerned. The Russian experiments exploring an entirely different idea of *découpage* were soon considered outdated or at best only marginally important. "Jump cuts" and "bad" or "unclear" matches were to be avoided because they made the essentially *discontinuous* nature of a shot transition or the *ambiguous* nature of cinematic space too apparent (the overlapping cuts in *October* were viewed as "bad" matches, and the *découpage* of Alexander Dovzhenko's *Earth* was thought to be "obscure"). Attempting thus to deny the many-sided nature of the cut, film-makers eventually had no well-defined aesthetic reason whatsoever for cutting from one shot to the next, often doing so for reasons of pure convenience, until by the end of the 1940's some of the most rigorous directors (Luchino Visconti in *La Terra trema*, Alfred Hitchcock in *Rope*, Michelangelo Antonioni in *Cronaca di un amore*)[9] began wondering whether cuts were necessary at all, whether they should not be purely and simply eliminated or used very sparingly and endowed with a very special function.

The time has now come to change our attitude toward the function and nature of cinematic articulation, both between individual shots and in the film over all, as well as its relation to narrative structure. We are just beginning to realize that the formal organization of shot transitions and "matches" in the strict sense of the word is the essential cinematic task. Each articulation, as we have seen, is defined by two parameters, the first temporal, the second spatial. There are, therefore, fifteen basic ways of articulating two shots, that being the number of possible combinations of the five temporal types and the three spatial types of transitions. Each of these possibilities, moreover, can give rise to an almost infinite number of permutations, determined not only by the extent of the time ellipsis or reversal but also, and more importantly, by another parameter that is capable of undergoing an almost infinite number of variations too: the changes in camera angle and camera-subject distance (not to mention deliberate discrepancies in eye-line angles or matching trajectories, which are less easy to control but almost as important). I am not saying that these are the only elements that play a role in a transition between shots. But other elements such as camera and subject movement, frame content and composition, and the like can define only the particular nature of a given match and not the function of articulations in general. As regards the content of the film image, it may be interesting to know that a close-up of a man's expressionless face followed by a shot of a bowl of soup creates the impression that the man is hungry; but this relationship between the content of two shots is a *syntactical* one that merely helps us determine the *semantic* relationship between them. Although film remains largely an imperfect means of communication, it is nonetheless possible to foresee a time when it will become a totally immanent object whose semantic function will be intimately joined with its plastic function to create a *poetic function*. Although camera movements, entrances into and exits from frame, composition, and so on can all function as devices aiding in the organization of the film object, I feel that the shot transition will remain the basic element in the infinitely more complex structures of the future.

One of the possible forms that this over-all organization of film articulations might take can already be foreseen, for the fifteen types of shot transitions can give rise to patterns of *mutual interference*, resulting in yet another controllable set of permutations. At the moment of transition, the articulation between two shots might seem to fit into any one of the five temporal categories and any one of the three spatial categories, but then something in shot B or some other subsequent shot might *retrospectively* reveal that the transition actually belongs in an altogether different temporal or spatial category, or perhaps even both. Examples of this procedure exist even in relatively conventional film-making. In a scene in Hitchcock's *The Birds*, Tippi Hedren, who has lingered too long at the home of the local schoolteacher, telephones her fiancé. The first shot shows her

The Birds

a

b, c

in a medium close-up. The next shot shows the teacher starting to sit down in an armchair, blocking part of the frame at the beginning of the shot. Because of the alternation between shots to which we have become accustomed in similar scenes, and more importantly because of the absence of any other clue to the spatial orientation, we have the impression the camera is aimed at some other part of the set; hence there appears to be preservation of temporal continuity (Tippi Hedren continuing her conversation off screen) along with spatial discontinuity. When the teacher is finally seated, however, she reveals the part of the set in the background that she has previously blocked from view, and we see Tippi Hedren in a medium-long shot at the telephone. Spatial continuity had in fact been preserved as well (it is a matching shot from the same angle). Our first impression of the situation was an erroneous one, and we are belatedly forced to correct our initial misconception. This is a much more complex process of awareness, to say the least, than that implied in the "invisible" match. The exact nature of the relationship between the two shots remains vague for several seconds and becomes obvious only sometime after the transition has occurred. The variable duration of this interval may furnish another parameter.

Another frequently employed technique involves having a distant shot of someone followed by a closer one, with this second shot subsequently turning out to be occurring at some other time and perhaps even in some other place. Although this procedure is commonly used in flashbacks and time ellipses, it has hidden potentialities that allow more complex formal structures to be created (as in *Une Simple histoire*).

It is, however, important to note that this sort of disorientation presupposes a "coherent" spatial and temporal continuity, a previously created context built around immediately comprehensible relationships between shots.[10] A more systematic,[11] more structural use of the disorientation created by these "retroactive matches" would depend on establishing some sort of dialectical relationship between such matches and others that are immediately comprehensible, a dialectic in which the "deferred" match might perhaps still be an exceptional device but would no longer remain a gratuitous or merely stylistic "gimmick."

Still other possibilities can result from the nonresolution of these "open" matches, films that would have this very ambiguity as their basis, films in which the viewer's sense of "real" space would be constantly subverted, films in which he could never orient himself. Resnais's *Last Year at Marienbad* and Jean-Marie Straub's *Nicht Versöhnt*, especially in their use of indefinite time ellipses and reversals, already provide examples.[12]

I have just briefly outlined a set of formal "objects"—the fifteen different types of shot transitions and the parameters that define them—capable of rigorous development through such devices as rhythmic alternation, recapitulation, retrogression, gradual elimination, cyclical repetition, and serial variation, thus creating structures similar to those of twelve-tone music. None of this is as abstractly theoretical as might be imagined.

As early as 1931, Fritz Lang's masterpiece *M* was entirely structured around a rigorous organization of the film's formal articulations, starting with sequences in which each shot is temporally and spatially autonomous, with time ellipses and changes in location playing the obviously predominant role, then gradually and systematically evolving toward the increasing use of the continuity cut, finally culminating in the famous trial sequence in which temporal and spatial continuity are strictly preserved for some ten minutes. In the course of this progression a certain number of "retroactive matches" also occur, the most striking of which takes place when the gangsters leave the building in which they have captured the sadistic child-murderer. Lang repeats a shot, already used several times, of a housebreaker seen through the hole in the floor he has made to get into a locked bank. The thief asks for a ladder so he can climb out. A ladder is thrown down and he clambers out, only to discover that it is the police and not his gangster friends who are there waiting for him. We then realize that the time between the mob's departure and the arrival of the police has been completely skipped over in a time ellipsis, that instead of occurring immediately after the departure of the thief's pals this shot in fact happens a good deal later than we initially thought.

A more recent film, Marcel Hanoun's little-known masterpiece *Une Simple histoire*, is entirely structured around principles similar to the one I have been describing. Although these principles are arrived at in Hanoun's case in a purely empirical manner, they are nevertheless applied with utmost rigor. *Une Simple histoire* will be examined in detail in another chapter.

The contemporary film narrative is gradually liberating itself from the constraints of the literary or pseudo-literary forms that played a large part in bringing about the "zero point of cinematic style" that reigned supreme during the 1930's and 1940's and still remains in a position of some strength today. It is only through systematic and thorough exploration of the *structural* possibilities inherent in the cinematic parameters I have been describing that film will be liberated from the old narrative forms and develop new "open" forms that will have more in common with the formal strategies of post-Debussyian music than with those of the pre-Joycean novel. Film will attain its formal autonomy only when these new "open" forms begin to be used organically. What this principally involves is the creation of a truly consistent relationship between a film's spatial and temporal articulations and its narrative content, formal structure determining narrative structure as much as vice versa. It also implies giving as important a place to the viewer's disorientation as to his orientation. And these are but two of the possible multiple dialectics that will form the very *substance* of the cinema of the future, a cinema in which *découpage* in the limited sense of breaking a narrative down into scenes will no longer be meaningful to the real film-maker and *découpage* as defined here will cease to be experimental and purely theoretical and come into its own in actual film practice. It is this cinema of the future that the following pages will hopefully help to bring forth.

Notes

1. From the verb *découper*, "to cut into pieces."
2. As of 1966.
3. Two meanings of the word "shot" should be distinguished, depending on whether it is shooting or editing that is being referred to. During shooting a shot refers to whatever is filmed after the camera starts and before it stops; during editing it refers to whatever is included between two "cuts" or shot changes. Two words are in fact needed, but to my knowledge no language makes such a distinction.
4. See my remarks below on the "zero point of cinematic style."
5. That this is no more than a convention is quite amply demonstrated by an episode in the television series "The Man from U.N.C.L.E.," which consisted

of two separate actions cross-cut together; on the one hand we witnessed Ilya Kouriakin's misadventures as a prisoner of an Arab tribe, obviously extending over a period of several days, and, on the other hand, Napoleon Solo's adventures, taking place within a period of only a few hours.

6. This has only recently become apparent, principally because this kind of ellipsis has ceased to be systematically indicated by dissolves.

7. The principal ones have been mentioned here. Also worth mentioning is the rule about changing a camera angle by at least thirty degrees (or not at all), which stems from the perceptual nature of the matched shot change (see Chapter 3).

8. Also worth citing: the cutaway, the rule of the median line, and the manner in which actors' movements can be slowed down or speeded up so that long shots and close-ups of the same subject match (see Chapter 3).

9. It is worth pointing out that this preference for prolonged shots was subsequently abandoned by all three directors, corresponding (in Antonioni's case at least) to an increased awareness of the extremely important function a shot change can fulfill.

10. The author refers readers to Eisenstein's concept of the "montage unit" as set forth in Vladimir Nizhny, *Lessons with Eisenstein* (tr., Jay Leyda and Ivor Montagu [New York: Hill and Wang, 1969]), a book with which he was unfamiliar at the time of writing.

11. Bresson's *Une Femme douce*, which appeared just before the publication of this book, has a formal texture entirely based on this kind of match—and it indicates the limits inherent in a systematic use of "deferred" or "retroactive" matches.

12. Robbe-Grillet's *L'Homme qui ment* (*The Man Who Lies*) obviously goes much farther in this direction.

2

Nana, or the Two Kinds of Space

To understand cinematic space, it may prove useful to consider it as in fact consisting of *two different kinds of space:* that included within the frame and that outside the frame. For our purposes, screen space can be defined very simply as including everything perceived on the screen by the eye. Off-screen space is more complex, however. It is divided into six "segments": The immediate confines of the first four of these areas are determined by the four borders of the frame, and correspond to the four faces of an imaginary truncated pyramid projected into the surrounding space, a description that obviously is something of a simplification. A fifth segment cannot be defined with the same seeming geometric precision, yet no one will deny that there is an off-screen space "behind the camera" that is quite distinct from the four segments of space bordering the frame lines, although the characters in the film generally reach this space by passing just to the right or left of the camera. There is a sixth segment, finally, encompassing the space existing behind the set or some object in it: A character reaches it by going out a door, going around a street corner, disappearing behind a pillar or behind another person, or performing some similar act. The outer limit of this sixth segment of space is just beyond the horizon.

What role do these spatial segments play in the formal development of a film?

This question could be answered in the abstract, but it seems preferable to refer to a film that is a model of the exhaustive use of off-screen space and its systematic opposition to screen space, Jean Renoir's masterpiece *Nana*, a key film in the development of a cinematic language.

Beginning with its first great dramatic scene, when Muffat meets Nana, the entire visual construction depends on the existence not only of an on-screen space but also of an off-screen space that is fully as important. How is this sense of off-screen space established?

In *Nana*, as in any film, the spatial segments are defined first of all by entries into and exits from frame. More than half the shots in Renoir's film begin with someone entering the frame or end with someone exiting from it, or both, leaving several empty frames before or after each shot. Indeed, we might say that the entire rhythm of *Nana* depends on these exits and entrances, their dynamic role becoming all the more important in that, except for a half dozen or so dolly and pan shots (to which we shall return later), the film consists almost entirely of shots during which the camera does not move. Obviously only four of the six spatial segments previously described are brought into play to any important degree: the area behind the camera, the area behind the set, and, most importantly, those areas bordering screen space on the right and left. The upper and lower segments are used for entrances and exits only in a few rare shots taken from an extreme upward or downward angle or along a staircase. I have said that these segments are "defined" by movements into or out of frame. By that I simply mean that one or another of the spatial segments in question takes shape in the viewer's imagination every time an entrance or exit occurs into or out of that segment. Toward the beginning of the film, there is a shot in which Muffat, rushing toward Nana's dressing room, meets young Georges, Nana's new conquest, as he leaves her dressing room in a sort of ecstatic daze. The shot in which their paths cross is an extremely brief one, lasting barely a second. The two men, seen in a medium shot against a bare wall, are caught in mid-flight, Muffat entering left and Georges right; their paths cross like two arrows, without their even glancing at each other, and they exit on opposite sides of the screen. The essential part of the action in this shot (the trajectories of the two men) takes place *off screen,* although in such a brief span of time—the moment preceding and following each entrance and each exit—that it borders on the instantaneous; this action *simultaneously* defines the left and right segments of off-screen space.

Renoir also attempts to use exits and entrances as a way of defining the spatial area "behind the camera" and "behind the set," a rare practice at the time *Nana* was made. He brings this area into play almost as often as he does those spatial segments contiguous to the four frame borders. Entrances and exits, through doors located near the center of the frame, preceded or followed by an empty screen, frequently occur in the film (particularly in Renoir's treatment of Nana's grand salon and boudoir). It is thus principally the *empty frame* that focuses our attention on what is occurring off screen, thereby making us aware of off-screen space, for with the screen empty there is nothing as yet (or nothing any longer) to hold the eye's attention. Of course, an exit leaving an empty frame behind makes us aware of a certain definite area of off-screen space, whereas a shot that begins with an empty frame does not always allow us to foresee which side of the screen someone will suddenly enter from or even if anyone will enter at all (as my comments on Yasujiro Ozu later in this chapter will indicate). At the same time, the principles governing matching screen direction and camera angle are of some help to us in certain cases, mainly in those involving the eventual entry into frame of a character whose direction of movement has been hinted at in an earlier shot—which in *Nana* is, however, far from always being the case. In any event, as soon as a character has actually entered the frame, his entry *retrospectively* calls to mind the existence of the spatial segment from which he emerged. Conversely, as long as the frame remains empty, all of the surrounding space is appreciably equal in potential, and the spatial segment from which the character emerges takes on *specific* existence and *primordial* importance only at the actual moment the person enters screen space.

Renoir also introduces another innovation in his use of space: His actors exit by brushing past the camera much more often than was customary in 1925, thus defining the space located behind it. More generally, however, one might wonder how to "classify" exits *along a diagonal*, since ordinarily access to the space behind the camera involves passage through either right or left spatial segment, except in the relatively rare case when the character exits "through" the camera, blocking the lens, and then perhaps unblocking it in the following shot as he "comes out of the other side." Probably 99 per cent of all frame exits and entrances have a *dominant direction*, and this is obviously so in the case of any entrance or exit that takes the form of brushing past the camera. Only a device such as an exit through one of the frame corners in a shot taken from a strictly vertical downward angle is really ambiguous in this respect.

There is also the case of the character's head jutting out of frame as he stands up, whereupon he exits from the frame altogether, either to the left or to the right; this variation, however, brings the two separate segments into play *successively*, that segment bordering the upper frame line first, then that bordering either the left or right frame line. Obviously any "horizontal" combination of this sort may be used.

A second way in which a film-maker can define off-screen space involves having a character look off screen. In *Nana*, an entire sequence or some part of it (the principal example being the scenes at the race track) frequently starts with a close-up or a relatively tight shot of one character addressing another who is off screen. Sometimes the gaze of the character speaking is so intense, so fraught with meaning, that the character off screen (and therefore the imaginary space that he occupies) becomes as important as, if not more important than, the person who is visible in frame and the actual screen-space. Nana's servants are constantly sticking their heads through doors to find out what is going on in the space we cannot see behind them, and both the invisible space thus defined and the invisible persons who occupy it are at least as important as what the viewer actually sees on screen. Finally, looking toward the camera (which is not the same thing as looking directly into the lens, for this latter sort of gaze gives the illusion of being aimed at the viewer and not at the space behind the camera and is seldom used except in commercials and for theatrical asides) defines the space behind the camera where the object of this gaze presumably is located.

A third way of defining off-screen space, this time in relation to a stationary and silent shot, involves framing a character in such a way that some part of his body protrudes out of frame. The set itself, of course, extending as it necessarily does all around the frame, also brings off-screen space into play in a similar way, although in this case it is a totally nonfunctional way. Off-screen space is, after all, purely imaginary, and only something that is the particular and *principal* focus of attention can bring it into play. It is not until a disembodied hand enters the frame to pluck the egg cup out of Muffat's hands as he absentmindedly toys with it that we become consciously aware of off-screen space. Up until that moment, the Count's legs, extending out of sight beyond the lower frame-line, or the shelves that probably extend beyond to the left, do not concern us in the same way. It is important to realize that off-screen space has only an intermittent or, rather, *fluctuating* existence during any film, and structuring this fluctuation can become a powerful tool in a filmmaker's hands. Renoir was one of the first to have fully realized this. Shots in which a hand is thrust into frame occur frequently in *Nana*, as when a man's hand (his body being otherwise invisible) enters the frame to offer Nana a drink in the dance-hall scene. In a certain sense, what is involved here is a rather special case of a frame entrance. However, because much of the person's body remains off screen, the off-screen space is more emphatically present than if his entire body had suddenly appeared in frame. This third way of defining off-screen space includes yet another subdivision that is completely *static*—for instance, in the shot where Nana's head and torso are cut off vertically by the left frame line throughout her long discussion with Muffat in the dance hall.

Off-screen space may be divided into two other categories: It may be thought of as either imaginary or concrete. When the impresario's hand comes into frame to take the egg cup, the space he occupies and defines is imaginary—we do not know, for example, to whom this arm belongs. When in a subsequent shot the camera reveals the full scene, with Muffat and the impresario side by side, the space becomes concrete *retrospectively*. A similar process occurs in any situation involving the use of shot and reverse shot, with the reverse shot converting an off-screen space that was imaginary in the initial shot into concrete space. This off-screen space might conceivably remain imaginary if no wider shot, no shot taken from another angle, or no camera movement is introduced revealing the person to whom an arm belongs, to whom an off-screen glance is directed, or the exact off-screen segment toward which an exiting character has headed. (The anonymous arm in the dance-hall scene is an example, for we never see whose arm it is, or the space that this person occupies, at least not explicitly.)

By contrast, in the remarkable scene in which Vandeuvre comes to Nana to chide her for her relations with young Georges, the transition from a medium shot of the two of them sitting side by side to a long shot showing the Count sitting by himself in the same place at the extreme right of the frame evokes an off-screen space that is altogether concrete in nature, for just prior to this shot we could see that Nana was sitting less than two feet from him, just beyond the edge of the new frame. Moreover, the Count continues to look in Nana's direction and continues to talk to her, thereby causing us to be very much aware of this fragment of off-screen space. Although the Count does rise and pace back and forth frame center, his chair remains where it was, and the preceding shot had clearly established that it is next to Nana's; we therefore continue to be quite conscious of this off-screen space. But we are soon to discover that this space has undergone a change without our knowing it. We think we are quite familiar with this space; we believe we know Nana's exact position and therefore precisely which section of space off screen right she occupies as Vandeuvre strides back and forth across the carpet. He finally exits right and then joins her in the next shot, entering this space from the left; the shot reveals that Nana in the meantime has sprawled out on a couch we had not previously seen (at least not in this sequence, which amounts to the same thing, so immense is our capacity for forgetting things during a film;[1] for this reason the structuring—and restructuring —of cinematic space can be achieved only within the limits of one particular sequence). We realize in retrospect that our initial conception of this off-screen space was erroneous, that the space being established was not what we thought it was, that it was, to use the terms of this discussion, not concrete but *imaginary*.

It should be apparent by now that we are once again dealing with one of the dialectical[2] dimensions of film form. Moreover, it is of some interest to establish parallels between this kind of retrospective awareness of the true nature of off-screen space and the delayed awareness of the spatiotemporal nature of a match. It is a dialectic in which a number of extremely complex possibilities are implicit, particularly when we consider that not only does the use of such devices as movements into or out of frame, off-screen glances, and partial framing (or the use of any two or three of these simultaneously) determine whether the space in question is imaginary or concrete but also that this space can be either predictive and imaginary or retrospective and concrete (through the use of spatial "ellipses" similar to the one just described in *Nana*, for instance), all quite independently of the spatial segment or segments actually brought into play, this latter factor multiplying the possibilities enormously in and of itself. But this ambiguity can also apply to the relationship of screen space and off-screen space itself. It is possible to see off-screen space without our being aware that it is off screen (as when the camera is aimed at a mirror with the mirror frame not visible), realizing that fact only after the camera pans or after someone in frame has moved. It is also possible to assume that someone or something present in a previous shot is somewhere off screen in the shot we are now viewing, whereas the person or object is actually in frame, but concealed by the play of shadows or colors (examples may be found in Ozu's *Duckweed Story* and Valerio Zurlini's *Cronaca familiare*). Obviously this happens relatively rarely and involves a paradox, almost a play on words (it being by definition impossible to "see" off-screen space). But it is important to be aware that inversions of this sort are possible (although perhaps occurring in some other form), because this helps establish the limits within which this particular parameter can evolve.

One might perhaps wonder what purpose an analysis of the kind I am undertaking can possibly have. Even if it is readily conceded that systematic oppositions of off-screen and screen space constituted one of Renoir's essential tools and that a film made over forty years ago is a success largely because of this opposition, any attempted classification of the possible relationships between these two kinds of space is nonetheless apt to be considered sterile and pedantic today. Have I not simply been describing how *every* film is made? Any film, admittedly, employs movements into and out of frame; any film, admittedly, suggests an opposition between screen space and off-screen space through the use of such devices as off-screen glances, the shot and the reverse shot, partially out-of-frame actors, and so on. Yet, from *Nana* on, only very few directors (the greatest ones) have used this implicit dialectic as an explicit means of structuring a whole film. At this point a clarification is in order. If *Nana* seems such an important film today, it is not merely because it marks the beginning of the extensive use of off-screen space but, more importantly, because it marks the first *structural* use of it. For many years the silent film regarded as using off-screen space most significantly was Ewald André Dupont's *Variety*. Why? Because during a fight scene that soon became famous, Emil Jannings and his rival roll on the ground, leaving the screen momentarily empty. A hand with a knife in it then enters the frame from below and immediately plunges out of frame again to deliver the fatal blow. Jannings then rises up and into frame all by himself . . . and several generations of film historians applauded this "magnificent understatement." From that moment on, off-screen space came to be used almost exclusively as a way of *suggesting* events when directors felt that simply showing them directly would be too facile. Erected into a veritable aesthetic system, this principle was carried to its ultimate limits in Nicholas Ray's first (and best) film, *They Live by Night*. In this gangster movie, all violence systematically occurred off screen or was simply "elided," thus creating what was undeniably a very odd sort of "intense understatement." However, this rather crude distinction between what is actually visible and what is left unseen utterly fails to take into account the complex vectors that *directional* and *diversified* oppositions between screen space and off-screen space can provide in the way of an aesthetic tool, as certain other directors had discovered.

Yasujiro Ozu, one of the greatest of pre–World War II Japanese directors, was the first film-maker after Renoir to have understood how important the existence of two distinct kinds of space is. He was also perhaps the first director to have really understood the value of the empty screen and the tensions that result from leaving it empty.

Although Renoir often has his actors in *Nana* move into or out of an empty shot, the screen remains empty for no more than a few frames, just long enough for the actor to make a definite entrance or exit. A certain visual monotony admittedly results from Renoir's frequent use of this technique, even though its repeated use does play a primary structural role in this masterpiece, as I have already pointed out. Ozu was doubtless the first to vary the *relative length of time* in which the screen was left empty, sometimes leaving it empty before an entrance, but more frequently after an exit. He began to use this procedure extensively in his last silent film, *Duckweed Story* (1935), and, even more importantly, in his first sound film and masterpiece, *The Only Son* (1936). It unfortunately became a kind of tic in many of the last works of his old age, which are, on the whole, more academic and stilted than his earlier, prewar films.

In *The Only Son*, the empty screen is used as a means of creating a whole maze of off-screen spaces, often made concrete in an entirely original way by showing some purely decorative, almost abstract, nonlocalized detail within the set or location, these shots generally occurring just after someone has exited from a shot or before a character enters the next shot. Ozu's use of this technique reaches a pinnacle in a relatively wide-angle shot (about a medium shot), following a perfectly conventional dialogue scene, in which the camera focuses on a fairly nondescript corner of the set for nearly a minute! Throughout this prolonged shot, a series of discrete off-screen sounds suggests all sorts of vaguely possible off-screen action, finally modulating into the noise of a factory and bringing on the next scene, which takes place in a vacant lot next to the factory whence the sounds are coming. This amazing shot quite clearly illustrates a basic principle: The longer the screen remains empty, the greater the resulting tension between screen space and off-screen space and the greater the attention concentrated on off-screen space as against screen space (the time required to exhaust our attention depending on how simple a scene the screen shows, a perfectly black or white screen constituting the obvious limit). Throughout *The Only Son* and his other films immediately following it, Ozu uses this tension as a variable parameter, the duration of empty screen shots varying from several twenty-fourths of a second to quite a few seconds. The variations in tension thus created provide him with a formal means of structuring his *découpage*. Their range is enormous and perfectly perceptible to the practiced eye.

Another film-maker for whom the empty screen and the off-screen space it establishes have a crucial importance is Robert Bresson. This is particularly obvious in A *Man Escaped* and *Pickpocket*. The shot in *A Man Escaped* in which Fontaine kills the sentry is a quite striking example. A rather tight shot shows Fontaine in three-quarter profile hugging the wall just short of the corner, on the other side of which the sentry is standing. Mustering all his courage, Fontaine moves forward, exits frame right, immediately circles around and re-enters, crosses the frame again, and re-exits to the left just beyond the corner of the wall. The screen now remains empty and quite neutral as the sentry is presumably killed (there is no sound from off screen, however), and then Fontaine enters once again.[3] Just as in the shot where Georges and Muffat cross each other's path in *Nana*, what we have here is a situation that essentially depends on bringing off-screen space into play, but in a complex and "syncopated" manner. This and other similar uses of off-screen space might be ascribed to Bresson's alleged reluctance to show distasteful scenes, but, as *Au Hasard Balthazar* and *Mouchette* have demonstrated, in actual fact he is not all that squeamish, and plastic values have always been the crucial ones determining his use of a technique, as is amply proved by the manner in which he organized the movements into and out of frame in this particular shot.

In *Pickpocket* the empty screen plays a much broader role. Here, Bresson achieves what might be called an orchestration of space, rigorously controlling the moments when the screen is left empty and the duration of these moments and establishing the precise extent of the surrounding off-screen space through his use of sound (the shots in which the pickpocket leaves his room, then exits from frame, with the sound of his footsteps then being heard as he makes his way down the stairs come particularly to mind).

Generally speaking, there are cases, especially in the silent film, where the relative length of time during which the screen is left vacant either before or after an exit or entrance itself determines, *independently of sound*, how large an area of off-screen space is established, even though this off-screen space may never actually be seen. The same holds true for the glance of anyone in frame looking toward someone off screen, whether the latter is standing still or moving. Off-screen sound, however, *always* brings off-screen space into play, regardless of whether or not it occurs in conjunction with any of the spatial modalities thus far described. When sound alone is involved, either as background noise, music, or an off-screen voice coming from an undetermined direction, it brings the surrounding space as a whole into play. Even when there is no indication of the *direction* a sound is coming from (and today, of course, stereophonic sound, on a strictly auditory level, provides *some* indication of direction), we are able to tell approximately how far away it is, and this *distance* factor provides yet another parameter, though it is one that as yet has seldom been explored.

Thus, whether through the use of sound, through the variation of the length of time the screen is left empty, or by means of off-screen glances, it is possible not only to bring now one and now another of the six spatial segments into play but also to indicate the extent of the off-screen space. The "unit" for measuring it, though indirect, is quite precise: One may not be able to determine that an off-screen actor is exactly thirty feet from the frame line, but it can be determined that it takes him four seconds, or else twenty frames, to reach it, and that fact makes it possible to control this particular parameter.

Michelangelo Antonioni is another great orchestrator of movements into and out of frame, particularly in his first film, which remains his masterpiece, *Cronaca di un amore*. It has often been noted that there are only two hundred or so separate shots in the entire film; most of them are very long, and all of them give proof of an absolutely unprecedented degree of visual organization. The principal structural factor in the film is movements into and out of frame, used mainly for rhythmic effect but also serving to bring into play, in an extremely complex manner, the spatial segments immediately adjacent to the frame lines, particularly those on the right and left. The bridge party sequence comprising two or three shots and running for some three minutes is built around Clara's repeated entries and exits, on the one hand, and those of a plump, ludicrous-looking woman with her dog cuddled in her arms, on the other. Because of the camera movements and the characters' movements off screen, these entrances and exits always occur at unexpected places and unexpected moments. In other sequences of the film, Antonioni often prolongs an exit by having someone on screen look off screen in the direction of a person who has just left, thereby bringing that segment of off-screen space to life. This is especially true in the admirable sequence shot of the lovers as they plan the murder on the bridge, a sort of elaborate circular pan, the lovers entering and exiting in turn, with these movements into and out of frame occurring at constantly varying distances from the camera, thus creating a hallucinatory rhythm underscoring the nature of the quarrel between the lovers, which simultaneously separates them and binds them together.

In his later films, Antonioni uses the empty frame quite extensively, in a manner somewhat reminiscent of Bresson. In *La Notte*, however, he introduces on several occasions a totally novel technique, whereby the "real" dimensions of whatever is visible on the empty screen are impossible to determine until the appearance of a human figure makes the scale obvious. As the husband goes up to the floor of the apartment building he lives on, for instance, the first thing we see is some kind of corrugated surface, the actual size of which is impossible to determine. When he then steps into the shot through the elevator door (which is not identifiable as such before it opens), his entrance not only leads to a change in the nature of the off-screen space (the spatial segment "behind the set" being specifically brought into play), but also modifies the actual area defined by the shot, for the space suddenly proves to be much smaller in scale and the camera much closer than had been apparent when the screen was still empty. Later, lying stretched out on a couch waiting for his wife to return, Marcello Mastroianni raises his eyes and looks out of the window (off screen). A shot of some sort of rectangular surface follows. His previous eye movements suggest that this surface, of as yet undetermined scale, is something he is looking at through the window, but when Jeanne Moreau walks into this new shot at the very bottom of the frame she looks very tiny. We then realize that the rectangular surface is actually the huge façade of some windowless, multistoried building. These two instances in which the awareness of the true scale of a shot does not occur until some time after it has begun are obviously analogous to the examples of the "retroactive" or "deferred" match described in Chapter 1.

A third method used by Renoir as a means of linking together screen space and off-screen space consists of framing only a part of an actor's body. This technique has become banal today as a way of situating a reverse angle shot (for instance, the back of a head on the edge of the screen); but, at the same time, the Japanese in particular have used it to create admirable effects of composition, obviously inspired by traditional Japanese graphic art.[4]

One other problem we must consider is camera movement, deliberately left for the last here, because it is much more resistant to analysis in terms of "two kinds of space" than are static shots. To return to *Nana*, there are, as I have already pointed out, only a half dozen or so camera movements in the entire film; therefore, their appearance tends in each instance to be a very special occasion. Only in two cases, however, do they seem to have been explicitly conceived of in terms of relating on-screen space to off-screen space. The first instance is a long dolly backward, starting from the pillows on Nana's bed,[5] with the camera gradually revealing her enormous boudoir as it backs away, off-screen space being involved here precisely because the function of the shot is to reveal the part of the room that was initially invisible. The second instance is the shot in which the camera tilts slowly up from Muffat's legs to reveal his full torso as he discovers Georges's dead body.

Any camera movement obviously converts off-screen space into screen space or vice versa. This is not the essential purpose, however, of all camera movement. It is often used to create what is essentially a *static composition* around one or several moving actors, as in the shot in Orson Welles's *Othello* in which the camera dollies backward following Iago and Othello as they walk on the ramparts, off-screen space coming into play only when Iago gets ahead of Othello and exits before him.

It is perhaps because the Russians, Alexander Dovzhenko in particular, sensed the multiple implications present in camera movements (only two of their many possible functions have been illustrated) that in some of their films they severely limited them and thereby made their use all the more striking. In Dovzhenko's *Earth* the few camera movements perceptible as such involve only slight "nudges" of the camera, which very explicitly reveal an off-screen space directly adjacent to the space in the original composition. I feel that, if a rigorously dialectical relationship between off-screen space and screen space is to be created, camera movements should participate in it in the manner suggested by the early Russians. Not that camera movements need always be as rare as they are in *Earth* (or in *Nana*), nor need they always participate in the spatial dialectic—thus suggesting yet another possible dialectic, that between camera movements that actually participate in the creation of some relationship between the two kinds of space and those that do not.

It is interesting to compare this notion of placing striking limitations on the use of camera movement with the formal conception underlying that other masterpiece of the French silent film, Marcel L'Herbier's *L'Argent*. This film, made in 1927, was the first to systematically use camera movement to establish the basic rhythm of the film's *découpage*, thereby anticipating by twenty years Welles's and Antonioni's film styles at their most sophisticated. Enormous stylized sets designed by Lazare Meerson invite L'Herbier's camera to dolly around frequently, unfolding new vistas of off-screen space at every turn. Spatially, the film is in a constant state of flux; this, plus the fact that the editing of the film is fully as rigorous as the camera handling, gives it an altogether original dynamic dimension. And, though I persist in believing that an analysis of camera movement in terms of the "two kinds of space" is scarcely an easy task, a close reading of *L'Argent* might perhaps provide a key.

As we have seen, the possibilities of articulating the relationships between screen space and off-screen space in an orderly fashion, of organizing them structurally above and beyond the simple orchestration of movements into and out of frame (which in itself is very seldom attempted), are even more complex than were the possibilities implicit in the structuring of the spatiotemporal articulations between shots. These possibilities become even more complex when we consider that the articulations of imaginary and concrete space described above also have a part to play. The analysis herein of this vital parameter has perhaps not been as exhaustive as that of the types of shot transitions. Nevertheless, the two types of space could conceivably be articulated in accordance with the same "para-serial" principles applicable to shot changes (repetition, alternation, elimination, progressive proliferation, and so on). Although it is true that a thoroughgoing and fully organic structuring of an entire film on the basis of these principles exists at present only as a theoretical possibility, the work of a Bresson or an Antonioni[6] already indicates that someday such a plastic organization will no longer be a purely speculative notion.

Notes

1. And my own capacity for making up things after the film is over. A student of mine has recently pointed out that the scene is much simpler than this, that in fact Nana never moves. I have left this false description in nevertheless, as the idea it illustrates still seems to me important, and as I am sure one could find—or make!—a sequence to bear it out. (See also the false example from Bresson's *A Man Escaped* in this same chapter.)
2. My notion of a dialectical film form developed several years before I had read Eisenstein's essential text "A Dialectical Approach to Film Form" in *Film Form*. Rather than cross swords with those Marxian film specialists who have upbraided me for my "irresponsible" use of the dialectical idea, I refer them to Eisenstein's analysis.
3. This description too is completely inaccurate. Fontaine actually only exits from frame once. I became aware of this during a re-viewing of the film just before submitting the final draft of the French manuscript. I nevertheless decided to leave this passage unchanged, thereby providing a deliberate example (there are doubtless inadvertent examples elsewhere in the text) of the viewer's faulty recollection of a film, a phenomenon quite intimately related to the way in which he perceives a film, which is a subject that deserves thorough study in itself. Aside from the problems it can create for a critic or analyst of films, I would like to point out the very positive effect this sort of faulty recollection can have on the creative faculty. The shot as it is described here does in fact exist in a short film made by myself, in which I incorporated the shot, as I remembered it, as an "homage" to Bresson.
4. Some compositions of this sort (the love scenes in *Hiroshima mon amour* and *Une Femme mariée*, for example) bring off-screen space into play only to a very slight degree (more so, however, than if the whole body were visible in frame). Moreover, there could conceivably be similar situations in which the viewer's awareness of off-screen space is momentarily intensified by having one of these "sculptural fragments" suddenly move, leaving the frame entirely, or having the rest of the body move into frame with it— which suggests yet another dialectical possibility.
5. These pillows are first seen in a mask shot that opens out as the dolly begins. The mask shot and the iris, even though infrequently used nowadays (see, however, François Truffaut's *Jules and Jim* and Charles Laughton's *The Night of the Hunter*), provide a very interesting way of transforming certain sections of screen space into off-screen space. In the light of the dialectical perspective proposed here, these techniques might recover their rightful place.
6. One might also add Vera Chytilova's admirable *O necem j iném* (*Something Different*); this film would have provided just as apt a chapter title as Renoir's *Nana*.

3

Editing as a Plastic Art

Thus far, I have examined the general nature of a filmed image and the articulations between such images without really considering what they actually look like. While still maintaining my "structural" approach, I might now examine both the image and the shot transition as concrete visual phenomena.

The Screen Image

I might first venture to point out how the way in which we see differs from the way in which a camera sees, an ambitious and somewhat risky endeavor, which many others, notably Karel Reisz in his excellent *Technique of Film Editing*,[1] have undertaken before me. However, since I am attempting to redefine the components of film form, I cannot avoid dealing with this particular problem, despite the difficulty involved.

We may approach it by considering a phenomenon that occurs as frequently in film as in real life: reflections on a glass surface. Let us see what the top of a pinball machine looks like when viewed from an angle. If the intensity of light on both sides of the sheet of glass is more or less equal, we will have no trouble making out what is taking place below it, and, if we are absorbed in a game in progress, we will see only that game; the glass will seem perfectly transparent. If, however, it should occur to us to examine the sheet of glass more objectively, we will notice that a reflection of the surroundings is superimposed on our view of the game going on underneath it, that both images are more or less equal in intensity, and that if the reflected image of the surroundings is at all complex the game in progress under the glass surface will now strike us as being practically "illegible." It is actually an unconscious mental process (selection) and a physiological process (focusing the eye) that enable us to differentiate successfully the two superimposed images, rejecting the one that does not interest us.

Let us now film this same situation without taking any special precautions. The resulting film image will show these two images superimposed, and when this superimposition is projected on the screen, we would succeed in eliminating the image that in principle does not interest us only with the greatest difficulty. The image of the game in progress beneath the glass would have become absolutely "illegible." If we wish to re-create the same effect we experienced watching the scene with the naked eye, we must attach a polarizing filter to the front of the lens to tone down the reflection or mask the reflected background, if this is possible.

Why is it impossible to distinguish between these two images once they have been captured on film and projected on a screen? This is because everything projected on a film screen has exactly the same intrinsic "reality," the same "presence." Once projected on the flat surface of the screen, the two superimposed images become one and indissoluble, mainly because the screen has only two dimensions and therefore any shape projected on it is equally "present," just as much "before our eyes" as any other shape. Even the parts of the image that are out of focus are perceived as quite distinct, visible, tangible entities, as what might be called "clumps of fuzziness." Another example might clarify this even further. Let us consider the following situation: While setting up a shot, a director of photography notices that there is a lamp or some other prop behind an actor, perhaps even several yards behind him, but just above his head. Even if the object in the background is going to be shown in such soft focus that its contours will be very indistinct, the director of photography will insist that the lamp be moved, because it will seem to be growing out of the actor's head. And he is quite right. Were we to be confronted with the same scene in life or were we to stand in the same place as the camera, we would not be at all disconcerted by the lamp; it would not strike us as being some monstrous excrescence; we would probably not even notice it. Yet, on the screen, this juxtaposition of objects would immediately leap to the eye, for when we view a screen we see everything at once; every form and every contour seems equally prominent visually (while sometimes we are completely oblivious to the head of a person sitting just in front of us and blocking as much as a fourth of that same screen!). Because of this fact, the problem of "legibility" arises more commonly and above all in more specific terms when we are observing a film image than when we are observing a real-life situation.

Our contention that all the elements in any given film image are perceived as equal in importance obviously runs counter to a fondly cherished notion of nineteenth-century art critics later embraced by a number of twentieth-century photographers: the belief that the eye explores a framed image according to a fixed itinerary, focusing first on a supposed "center of compositional focus" (generally determined by the time-honored "golden rectangle"), then traveling through the composition along a path supposedly determined by the disposition of its dominant lines. Eisenstein himself was quite taken with this notion, and the visual portion of his analysis of the introduction to the battle on the ice in *Alexander Nevsky* is based on this supposition. Such a conception is as outdated in art criticism today as composition according to the golden rectangle is in the art of painting. Even if the nineteenth-century eye did indeed see things in this way, the modern eye apparently does not. Any film image obviously includes some elements that call attention to themselves more strongly than others do, a case in point being that someone who is speaking will generally be noticed first. This is indeed true, but we are nonetheless also aware of the compositional whole, of which the person speaking is but a part, and we are aware in particular of the actual rectangular frame, even if the background of the image is uniformly black, white, or gray. For to "look" has to do with a mental process, whereas to "see" has to do with the physiology of the eye. And, when we view a film, as when we view a painting or a photograph, *seeing* is no longer dependent on *looking*, as is nearly always the case in a real-life situation; the selectivity involved in looking no longer affects the nonselectivity involved in seeing in the slightest.[2]

For all this to be the case, there is, however, one essential condition: The viewer must be seated at the proper distance from the screen. If he is too close, so close that his field of vision does not include the whole screen, his eyes must change focus as the centers of visual interest shift, and he will never be able to grasp the total visual effect created by the framed image. If, on the other hand, he is too far away, the image will be so schematic that he will see only these centers of interest, within a frame that is smaller than that seen in the view-finder by the film-maker when he shot it (the view-finder image, we must remember, takes in the eye's whole field of vision), and the initial principles underlying the composition will thus be distorted (just as in painting, a particular composition cannot be successfully executed on every scale, each composition seemingly having a scale best suited to it). With these as well as other considerations being taken into account, it has been mathematically determined that the optimum viewing distance is approximately two times the width of the screen. The fact that under present circumstances it is quite impossible for every viewer in a theater to be at that precise distance from the screen (nor even within a reasonable approximation of it) does nothing to invalidate this principle, but simply indicates that the movie theaters of the future will have to be built differently.[3]

Once a film-maker has become aware of the nature of the film image, as outlined here, what conclusions should he draw? First, to state the obvious, the frame must always be conceived of as a total composition. Yet the possible ways of composing any given shot are as various as the temperaments of individual film-makers, and the problem of composition in general is beyond the scope of this book. On the other hand, a far smaller number of film-makers are aware of, let alone concerned with, the possibility—or even the obligation, if they are at all sensitive to the imperative need to deal organically with the raw materials of film-making—of organizing the transitions —that is, the articulations between shots as a function of the total composition of each successive shot—thereby creating a structural framework capable of incorporating the formal elements discussed thus far as well as those to be dealt with in future chapters.

Static Articulations

Generally speaking, the first film-maker to concern himself with abstract cinematic form as concretely embodied in "figurative" film-making was Sergei Eisenstein. And he is also one of the relatively few film-makers to have actually set down his formal preoccupations in writing.

Eisenstein's analysis of his first masterpiece, *The Battleship Potem-kin*, emphasizes the film's over-all structure, based on the five-act pattern of classical tragedy, on poetic caesura, and on the golden rectangle, first of· all; then, taking the well-known Odessa steps sequence of the film as his example, he discusses the plastic organization attained through editing.

The editing of this sequence, Eisenstein tells us, is based on oppositions between the dynamic content of the various shots (rapid movements as against slow movements, ascending movements as against descending movements) and on oppositions between shot sizes (and therefore between the number of objects and people included in each shot). The altogether extraordinary aesthetic tension of this historic film sequence is created through the interplay of these formal contrasts.

When he analyzes the religious procession in *The General Line*, Eisenstein introduces a new concept, which he calls "polyphonic montage," a kind of musical interweaving of the different "voices" of the sequence (enthusiasm, ecstasy, shots of men singing, shots of women singing); variations in shot size are also involved.

One of Eisenstein's greatest discoveries, which, however, he appears to have written about only incidentally, is his approach to editing as a function of the composition of each successive shot, particularly in situations involving a series of shots showing the same subject from a number of different angles.

To understand what this entails, we have only to recall a school of painting that originated only a few years before Eisenstein shifted his artistic preoccupations from painting to theater and cinema. I am referring, of course, to Cubism, and more particularly to an aspect of Cubist experimentation best typified, perhaps, in the various studies of stringed instruments undertaken by Juan Gris around 1912 (although examples from Italian futurism would also be relevant here). If we examine a painting such as *Violin and Guitar* (1913), we find that what may be regarded as the central motif is made up of three tightly "framed" representations of the fingerboard and, between two of these, a "close-up" of the sounding-board. And, while it would be greatly oversimplified to reduce the painting to this multiple view of an object, to the extent that this motif *is* that, it may be regarded as a premonitory illustration of the aesthetic strategy involved in cutting together shots of the same subject from different angles, as Eisenstein was to develop it some ten years later. Now, it may be postulated that part of the pleasure afforded by the Gris painting derives, not from simply seeing an object depicted from several viewpoints simultaneously, but rather from the process by which the eye compares each aspect with the others, identifying "objectively" common features in their new perceptual guise, setting differences against similarities—in short, discovering continuity in discontinuity, and vice versa. Now, because of the way in which the eye remembers shapes, two shots of the same subject taken from two different angles can result in the same sort of aesthetic satisfaction when they are intercut. More specifically, variations in contours or areas from one shot to the next—relative to the fixed coordinates provided by the frame lines—can set up a play of tensions and permutations that will be highly satisfying to the eye, thanks to their complexity and coherence, and also quite capable of being structured.

That there is a structural potential here is quite evident, though we must admit that the above-mentioned satisfaction is rather vague in nature. That this sort of pleasure does correspond to quite concrete factors seems to be confirmed by the existence of the so-called thirty-degree rule. This rule, empirically established during the 1920's, has it that any new angle on the same camera subject must differ from the previous angle by at least thirty degrees.[4] Film-makers had noticed that any angle change of less than thirty degrees (and thus not counting moving the camera closer or farther away with no change of angle—what the British call a "concertina") resulted in a "jump" that made the viewer vaguely uncomfortable. This feeling of malaise is doubtless due to the tenuous, ill-defined character of such a cut; the new shot is not sufficiently distinct from the preceding one, especially if both are taken from similar camera-subject distances. Yet one could just as easily say that this discomfort results from the utter visual pointlessness of this kind of cut, that the viewer's feeling of vague annoyance stems mainly from the fact that his eye is frustrated, for it demands that, if there is any change at all in the configuration that it sees, this change must be a noticeable one and the resulting tensions must be pronounced and obvious.

We might briefly point out that, although this rule teaches us something very important about the nature of a shot change, it nonetheless is not sacrosanct; changing the angle by less than thirty degrees has already become part of the modern film-maker's vocabulary, for, as we have already indicated in our discussion of eye-line matches and screen-direction matches, malaise or discomfort can provide an altogether useful element of tension, as is demonstrated by Godard's *Breathless* and many of Sam Fuller's films, which abound in jump cuts, usually occurring at moments of extreme violence.

We have said that Eisenstein was probably the first film-maker to have conceived of frame composition as a function of the over-all relationship between a film's separate images. In *October*, the series of low angle shots of the cathedral towers consists of simple reversals of diagonal lines, while the sequence of the suspended bicycles employs a simple but very attractive set of variations on gleaming round forms set against a black background. *The General Line* contains a series of ultra-rapid flashes of the cream-separator's spout creating spatial relationships that are somewhat more complex in nature, involving contrasts between the spout seen with a more or less pronounced degree of foreshortening and the same spout seen "undistorted" in full profile. Equally effective albeit more elementary are the multiple reversals of direction of a train of carts being towed through the fields by the all-powerful tractor. But perhaps the most perfect example of this method of spatial recomposition is to be found in the opening sequence of Eisenstein's suppressed film *Bezhin Meadow*. The sequence centers around the body of a dead woman lying prone on a cart as her son weeps for her and the father

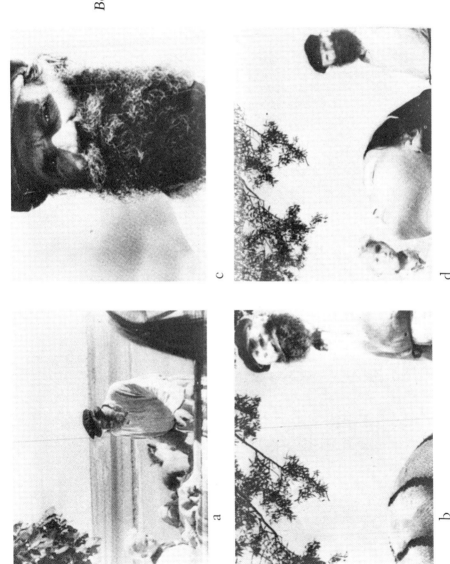

Bezhin Meadow

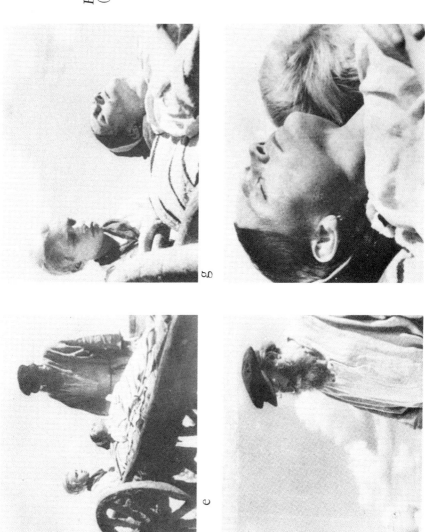

The sequence is complete, as it appears in the posthumous version of the film, except for two titles, a repeated close-up, and a cutaway shot of the horses.

i

k

j

l

stands looking on. Each of the elements of this "tableau" recurs in every succeeding shot, yet they have been so radically rearranged each time they reappear as to constitute a totally new variation on the initial space. Unfortunately, it is quite impossible to analyze this sequence in great detail, for the film has come down to us only in the form of the frame enlargements that are all that remain of it. Yet we may still perhaps regard it as Eisenstein's mature achievement in this particular direction. *Ivan the Terrible*, on the other hand, contains interesting contrasts of a quite different sort. The scene in which the boyars are waiting for news of Ivan's hoped-for death opens with three close-in shots of small groups of anxious faces. In the background of each shot is the same brightly lighted icon, differently placed in the frame. There is similarity of composition with respect to the figures, dissimilarity with respect to the icon. It is fairly clear that these shots in no way "match" among themselves (the relative positions of the figures and the icon have obviously been tampered with to achieve satisfactory recombinations from shot to shot). Such tampering violates one of the sacrosanct rules of spatial "continuity," and usually it results in that sense of disorientation and malaise that we have discussed. But this is not at all the case here. Why? Simply because Eisenstein has here managed to create a very unusual sort of cinematic space: It exists only in terms of the totality of shots included in the sequence;[5] we no longer have any sense of a surrounding space endowed with independent existence from which a sequence of shots has somehow been excerpted. Rather, we see a space that exists in the same many-faceted, complex way that Braque's billiard table exists; we see a setting that is the sum total of all the perspectives of it embodied in the successive shots, a setting whose cohesion is created by the harmonious articulation of the shots. This obviously is a rare and difficult achievement. Several similar "bad" matches in Ivan's "death chamber" used for analogous compositional reasons (they stem mainly from a concern with the pictorial harmony of each individual shot) merely create a feeling that something is "wrong." The spatial unity of the room is too definitely established before and after these isolated matches for us to feel that they are anything but gratuitous violations of that unity. Yet the previously described shots of the boyars show the way, suggesting how shot spaces can be coherently articulated so that space becomes "open," and proving that the more carefully planned the permutations of objects from shot to shot are, the more apparent this "openness" will be.

Akira Kurosawa is one of a number of contemporary film-makers who have been strongly influenced by this concept. This is most clearly apparent in the first part of his remarkable *High and Low*. For about an hour, the action unfolds almost entirely within a rich industrialist's bay-windowed living room, where a manhunt for the kidnaper of the son of the industrialist's chauffeur is being organized. The wide screen serves to emphasize the principle of visual organization implicit in most of the "matches," based as they are on constant variations in the screen positions of the many characters from one shot to the next: the industrialist, his family, his servants, and police officers, present either all together or by turns in the room. These permutations, moreover, are often combined with a process of selection. In a first shot we might have, for instance, from left to right, characters A, B, C, and D. In the succeeding shot, by choosing the proper camera angle and tampering a bit with actual positions, we might have D at the extreme left of the screen, B at the extreme right, and everyone else off-screen. C, B, and A might then reappear in the subsequent shot in this new order from left to right, and so on. Kurosawa's treatment of people as *interchangeable units*, a conception that goes far beyond the conventional notions of matching screen positions, allows a rather elaborate, almost serial organization of shots, an organization that provides the actual spoken dialogue as it unfolds with a base line, so to speak, either underlining it or counterpointing it in a manner that might be described as dialectical.

Let us go back in film history once again and refer to yet another example of a visual organization based on the permutability of similar or identical shapes—in this case again the human body, which functions as a constant, regardless of what individual character is on screen at any given moment. This principle of organization can be seen in the first part of *Boule de suif*, Mikhail Romm's first film (1934), set entirely within a particularly restricted space, the inside of a stagecoach. In order, doubtless, to avoid the visual monotony inherent in such a situation as this, where half a dozen people are riveted to their seats carrying on a conversation (which, moreover, is soundless, since this is one of the last films of the silent era), Romm relies on a *découpage* in which very few shots are ever repeated, in itself a remarkable achievement and one that reveals how aware Romm was of the need for a constant variation of visual space. Not only does he constantly vary the identity, size, eye-line direction, and number of faces in each shot; he also continually counterpoints faces shown in sharp focus and faces shown in soft focus: At times a face shown in close-up, screen right, may be in sharp focus while two faces in the background remain in soft focus, at times a face in the background in the center of the frame may be in sharp focus while two faces only partly in frame are in soft focus, and so on. The variations that may result when this parameter interacts with the four cited above are obviously enormous, and Romm takes full advantage of them.[6]

Thus far I have discussed only the visual relationships between shots involving an actual cut, situations, that is, in which our eye recalls what it saw in shot A and compares it with what it sees in shot B; the structural tensions that result from such a comparison provide the essential justification for this type of editing. A dissolve, however, is fundamentally no different as a visual entity; it merely provides a slightly different way of juxtaposing two spatial compositions, for the momentary superposition of two images concretizes a visual relationship similar in most respects to the "imaginary" relationship existing between two shots linked by a straight cut. This fact is often forgotten now that the dissolve has become a "punctuation mark" capable of linking any two shots together so as to indicate the passage of time. However, such use of the dissolve is in fact a relatively recent convention.

When the dissolve was first discovered in the early years of silent film, it was used more freely; it rarely had any specific "meaning" and was hardly ever employed to indicate the passage of time. Because there were titles for that very purpose, dissolves were not needed. For many years in the silent era, dissolves were used as a means of securing a "soft transition" from a close-up to a long shot (or vice versa) within a single perfectly continuous sequence. More generally speaking, they were used to create plastic, rhythmic, or poetic effects (Abel Gance, Germaine Dulac, Jean Epstein, and Marcel L'Herbier providing notable examples of this). Even after the introduction of sound the dissolve continued to be used in a very free way for a variety of purposes. In *Applause* (1929), for example, Rouben Mamoulian used dissolves as a way of getting from a shot of a character on the telephone to a shot of the person on the other end of the line. It was not until a number of years later that the current convention whereby a dissolve invariably indicates a passage of time became firmly established.[7]

Several contemporary young directors have recently reacted against the overfacile use of this convention and simply eliminated dissolves altogether in many of their films (Godard, Resnais, Hanoun). Bresson, on the other hand, while seemingly continuing to assign a conventional meaning to dissolves, in fact uses them as a structural element, as both a rhythmic and a plastic entity, thereby adopting the silent film-makers' freer approach. What strikes one in this respect in his *Diary of a Country Priest, A Man Escaped,* and *Pickpocket* is Bresson's concern with making the dissolve into an autonomous formal device, using it as a means of concretizing the relationship between two compositions based on the same or identical materials as well as that between shots based on completely dissimilar materials. In *Pickpocket* particularly, the differences in angles from which the hand is seen stealing into a pocket as one image dissolves into another and the way in which the position of the hand shifts in the frame from one shot to the next are only a further development of the kind of editing discovered by Eisenstein and explored by Romm, Kurosawa, and others. There is, of course, an important difference in rhythm between a dissolve and a cut: In a dissolve, the superposition is not instantaneous and "imaginary" but occurs over a span of several seconds; it is less abrupt, flows more easily, and, above all, "occurs before our very eyes." But, on one level of phenomenological analysis, they are identical.

Before abandoning this discussion of the possible relationships created through "static matches," a word might be added about the juxtaposition of two totally dissimilar shots—two shots, that is, that have no similar visual elements. Is it possible to structure such a relationship other than "semiotically"? The problem involved here is a very delicate one. I feel that any plastic relationship resulting from the juxtaposition of two shots of this sort can be discussed only in terms of specific instances and cannot be analyzed in general terms, even in the vague way used above to analyze the possible articulations between shots that include some common elements. This is, however, a problem that every film-maker should be aware of and seek to resolve in his own particular fashion, even if only in a purely empirical and practical way.

Dynamic Articulations

In the preceding pages of this chapter I have restricted myself to a discussion of the possible ways of creating graphic relationships between shots that are essentially static at the moment that the cut is made. But one can also cut, of course, from one shot to the next when some essential part of one or the other of them is in motion. Is it possible to organize this type of shot change, either independently of the types of structures to which two completely static shots lend themselves or in conjunction with them? The principles governing these types of structures should be equally applicable to any two shots containing moving elements. The actors' movements in Kurosawa's *High and Low*, for instance, do not affect the structural principles previously outlined at all.

Once again, Eisenstein was the first to be concerned with this aspect of "dynamic cutting." We have already seen that one of the basic structural elements of the Odessa steps sequence in *The Battleship Potemkin* is the contrast between ascending and descending movements. In this case, however, the directions of real movements and of these movements as they appear on the screen correspond; the ascending movements of the people of Odessa making their way up and the descending movements of the soldiers coming down the steps are both filmed in such a way that these respective directions are faithfully reproduced on the screen.[8] In *Strike*, on the other hand, there is a series of shots showing how a group of mischievous workers send the spying foreman sprawling with a nudge from a heavy wheel dangling from the end of a crane. In the first shot the wheel swings from right to left; a second shot shows the same wheel moving in the opposite direction, and the foreman's fall is likewise seen from opposite angles. Eisenstein was well aware that this was a rather radical violation of the principles governing matching screen direction, but he nonetheless felt the need for linking these shots together in this way, without the insertion of cutaways, because of the aesthetic effect, the feeling of jarring, violent speed that results from this match.

Although an isolated instance at that period, it nevertheless pointed the way to the structures that might result from changing the screen direction of movements that are quite obviously continuous in what is supposedly the "reality" being filmed. In modern cinema, a striking example of a sequence of shots based on this principle occurs at the beginning of Jean-Pierre Melville's *Bob le flambeur*. Bob enters the Place Pigalle early in the morning, and, as he walks through it, he is seen from several very different angles, each shot including a municipal water-sprinkling truck making its way around the square. Owing to the difference in angles, the sprinkler's direction of movement is not at all the same from shot to shot: At times it moves from left to right, at times from right to left, at times away from the camera, at times toward the camera, and the beauty of the sequence stems directly from this broken pattern, from these apparent shifts in screen movement as opposed to the real (or supposedly real—here too one must often cheat) trajectory that we automatically reconstruct in our minds. The apparent implication here is that a film audience's perception has somehow evolved from the time in which a change in screen direction was automatically equated with a change in real direction, a reaction that brought about the "rule" governing matching screen directions. In actual fact, however, the situation is not that simple. Just as *Ivan the Terrible* contains, as I have pointed out, apparent mismatches in screen position that perform a plastic function (and therefore do not "bother" us), as well as other matches that are jolting, so too "mismatches" in screen direction are a "valid" technique only when the accompanying sense of disorientation results in a perceptible structure. In the brilliant nymphomaniac sequence in *La Notte*, Antonioni shows the girl kicking the door of her room shut. But the latch does not catch, and the door abruptly swings back away from the camera. In the following shot, a close-up taken from inside the room, the door (cut on its movement) is now seen swinging back toward the camera again. This second shot could conceivably create the impression that the door had changed direction in "real" space. The actual trajectory of a door as it swings back is so familiar to us, however, that we have no trouble re-establishing the real nature of the

movement—we immediately apprehend it as one continuous movement that has been "rendered" as if it were discontinuous. These
two shots thereby stand out as the components of one of the two
strong matches around which the sequence pivots, the second being
the following match: a transition from a straight-on close-up centered on the girl to a medium shot in which she is on the far right
side of the frame, a transition completely ignoring the principles governing the "concertina" and resulting in a second abrupt break in
the flow of the sequence. It is worth pointing out the obvious analogies between the manner in which we apprehend the deliberately
omitted portion of a continual temporal process (ellipsis) and the
mental process that occurs when we compare a movement as it appears on the screen with that movement as we assume it occurred in
"reality." This, of course, is not the first analogy of this sort we have
come upon in the course of our analyses, nor will it be the last. Cor-
respondences of this kind doubtless indicate the fundamental cohe-
siveness of the various cinematic parameters as well as how these
parameters might eventually be organically interrelated to set up a
vast series of permutations so complex in nature as to be totally
beyond anything presently imagined.

Another type of dynamic articulation juxtaposes an internally
static image at the end of one shot with an image in motion at the
beginning of the subsequent shot. Flashes of static shots alternating
with extremely rapid tracking shots, a technique some members of the
French avant-garde of the 1920's were extremely fond of, is a rather
crude example of this type of structure; Orson Welles's version of
Othello is an altogether more satisfactory one. A large number of
scenes in the film are built around cuts involving the following two
types of shots: A first shot may show a motionless actor who suddenly begins to move just before the shot ends, only to be seen
standing still once again in the second shot without having completed the movement he has previously begun, this movement's final
phase having been abridged in the transition; or, in another variant,
an actor might be completing a movement at the beginning of the
second shot, even though he was motionless at the end of the first.
When it occurs as frequently as it does in *Othello*, this type of transition creates a rather special rhythm and a very flexible structure
that can be varied by alternating the two sorts of matches or by a

threefold combination of these matches, straight continuity cutting, and other types of temporal abridgement. It goes without saying that this type of shot transition can be used in conjunction with the various sorts of static matches already described, as is often the case in this film.

Similar relationships between static and moving shots are also possible when they contain quite dissimilar elements; directors such as Juan-Antonio Bardem and Michael Cacoyannis have a predilection for this kind of shot change. But this technique seems too facile, not organic enough, too mechanical, when compared to shot changes involving "brief ellipses" in the action that add a "vertical" dimension to the "horizontal" opposition between the spaces defined by the two shots.

Thus far, we have discussed only one of the two vectors of movement: direction. There is also speed. Apparent screen speed varies in direct proportion to the camera's distance from the subject. If we film a man raising his hand in a medium shot, then film that man doing the same thing at the same speed in close-up, the gesture will now appear to be much faster than it was in the medium shot, for in the same time that it takes a hand in a medium shot to travel across a fraction of a foot of screen space, it will have traveled several feet of screen space in a close-up. Accepted practice, an expression of that "zero point of cinematic style" we have already mentioned, requires that the apparent screen speeds of two shots be matched by tampering with "real" speeds. Clearly we are dealing here again with a situation involving a discontinuity as opposed to a continuity, and the film-maker can in fact use these differences in apparent speed for dialectical purposes; in this instance as in all others involving cutting on movement it is not difficult to imagine how a dialectic of this sort could be combined with a dialectic of direction.

At this point, one can only note that the analysis contained in this chapter is a good deal less exhaustive, less systematic, and above all more pragmatic than the discussion in the last two chapters, perhaps because the subject dealt with here is far broader and much more intangible than the relatively simple questions of the spatiotemporal articulation of shots and the relation of off-screen space to screen space. It is extremely difficult to describe, much less classify, any of the phenomena we have been discussing in this chapter: Classification might not even serve any useful purpose in this context, for editing as a plastic art is so complex a subject that those of us concerned with film probably do not yet have the means with which to undertake serious analysis of it. For the time being, any investigation in this field must necessarily take a pragmatic form, the making of films. Contemporary and future film-makers who are aware of these problems will discover far more rewarding, more complex, and more rigorous ways of organizing "matches" functionally than any outlined here, and the examples cited here will then seem quite naïve in retrospect. But perhaps they will at least serve to open the discussion.

Notes

1. Karel Reisz and Millar Gavin, *Technique of Film Editing* (New York: Hastings, 1967).
2. What is described here, however, is the "good gestalt" of an ideal viewer. Further research has shown that the film-goer often tends to see filmed images very much as he sees life: unframed, *lumpen*, with the figures completely blotting out the ground. The pinball example is in fact an extreme case significant only on an elementary level.
3. These comments were written before the release of Tati's *Playtime*. Even if they still hold true for films in general, they are not applicable to Tati's film, the first in the history of cinema that not only must be seen several times, but also must be viewed from several different distances from the screen. In its form, it is probably the first truly "open" film. Will it remain an isolated experiment? Masterpieces somehow eventually assert their authority and become models.
4. In the Gris painting, it will be noted that this rule is "respected" only as regards the first and third representation of the violin (counting from the right): The difference in "framing" between the third and fourth images is minute; the difference factors are more specifically pictorial. I mention this in order to stress the limitations of any comparison between Eisensteinian editing and Cubist representation.
5. Carl Dreyer's *The Passion of Joan of Arc* is built entirely around this simple idea and constitutes a perfect introduction to this fundamental concept.
6. It is also worth noting that, in the film as a whole, there is a complete opposition between the first part and the second part, which takes place entirely inside an inn, the camera remaining rather distant from the action, the depth of field being kept at a maximum, very short focal-length lenses and low angles being used throughout, in anticipation of what was to be the characteristic style of the early Orson Welles films. Curiously enough, this split into two parts is not without analogies to *High and Low*, for the sec-

ond part of Kurosawa's film abandons the apartment in which the first part
of the action takes place and shifts to the streets and slums of Tokyo,
which change of setting brings about a radical change of style.

7. The reasons for this standardization are intimately bound up with the
establishment of the "zero point" of film-making defined earlier. This particular manifestation of that development would make a fascinating subject
of study from the point of view of film perception.

8. This is true only in part. Actually, this sequence is a large-scale development
of the concept of "montage units," that is, a dialectic of "good" and "bad"
matches, inaugurated in *Strike* and theorized by Eisenstein in his teaching—
see *Lessons with Eisenstein* by Vladimir Nizhny (New York: Hill and
Wang, 1962).

II

Dialectics

4

The Repertory of Simple Structures

Frequent mention has been made in the first part of this work of a dialectical conception of cinematic form. It must be emphasized once again that this is not so much a specifically Hegelian process as a conception principally and perhaps somewhat improperly borrowed from serial music, from what the contemporary French composer and theoretician Jean Barraqué has called post-Webernian "musical dialectics": the organization of the various musical parameters (pitch and duration of sound, instrumental attack, timbre, and even silence) within musical space. As has already been pointed out, cinematic parameters of a similar nature exist. Thus far, I have been concerned largely with examining the most important of these parameters from the point of view of *découpage* (the spatiotemporal characteristics of the match, the relationships between screen space and off-screen space, and plastic interactions between shots), the very nature of which suggests the possible forms that their dialectical organization might take. It might be pointed out in passing that there are still other parameters of this sort, obviously lending themselves to a similar sort of organization: variations in shot size, in camera angle and height, in direction and speed of camera and subject movement within the shot, and, naturally, in *the duration of a shot*. Duration, however, confronts us with a basic problem, if only

51

because an examination of it reveals, once and for all, the limits of
my analogy with serial music. For, while there are in fact general
analogies between the dialectics of serial music and those of film,
there is also a fundamental difference: the fact that these cinematic
dialectics cannot be expressed or written down in purely arithmetical
terms as musical structures ultimately can be. And yet, if there is one
cinematic parameter that would seem to be quite easily reducible
to its mathematical equivalent, it is the duration of a shot expressed
in seconds and frames. It has even been suggested that these time
spans could be built up into something like "tone rows." Nevertheless the daily experience of any film-maker (as well as the few spo-
radic attempts that have been made to organize the durations of
shots in patterns independently of their content) shows quite clearly
that the viewer's estimate of the duration of a shot is conditioned by
its *legibility*. Roughly speaking, it is a direct function of legibility; an
uncomplicated two-second close-up will appear to be longer than a
long shot of exactly the same duration that is swarming with people;[1] a white or black screen will appear to be longer still. For this
reason, the organization of *perceptible* durations is a process that in
the final analysis is as complex and necessarily as empirical as that of
organizing ellipses; and, for the same reason, any given cinematic
rhythmical pattern measured simply in seconds and frames will never
be experienced in the same way as a musical pattern, unless it consists of nothing more than a simple alternation of black and white
frames. If the images involved are at all complex, this rhythmical
unit remains little more than a pure abstraction and is not at all perceptible as a coherent pattern.

Despite this, the possible ways of structuring this double phenomenon of duration and legibility constitute a problem that every great
film-maker has tackled, each in his own way. Alain Resnais, perhaps,
has been the one most consciously concerned with it. He was probably the first to realize that the wide screen, rather than forcing the
film-maker to use only relatively prolonged shots (because of the
greater difficulty the viewer has "reading" each shot in this format),
on the contrary considerably *expands* the possible range of relationships between duration and legibility. In *Marienbad*, he deliberately
alternates very prolonged shots with very short shots, with some of

these latter involving flashes of only a few frames. In a more general way, Resnais is one of the few *auteurs* (together with L'Herbier, Eisenstein, and, above all, Gregory Markopoulos[2]) to have realized that the relationship between duration and legibility in itself constitutes a dialectic and that simply finding a duration adequate to the legibility of each shot is not what is important; the creative factor lies, rather, in varying the ease or difficulty with which a shot can be "read" by making certain shots too short to be "comfortably" grasped (thus creating a "tension" through frustration) or so long that they can be read and reread to the point of absolute satiety (thus causing a "tension" through boredom).[3] These constitute the poles (or rather the vectors) of a true dialectic of durations capable of generating visual rhythms ultimately as complex as those of contemporary music.

Besides these parameters having to do with the *découpage* of a film, other potentially dialectical parameters exist, which can, I think, be listed with some degree of thoroughness because they are so clearly bipolar in nature.

The first of these are the *photographic parameters*, the most important of which are perhaps softness and sharpness of focus, as well as their corollary, the extent of the depth of field. I have already dealt with the part these parameters play in the composition of Romm's *Boule de suif*. However, the first film-makers to have experimented with this theme to any appreciable extent were Germaine Dulac, Jean Epstein, Abel Gance, and Marcel L'Herbier, a group often referred to as the French impressionists or first French avant-garde. Their concern with contrasts in focus led them to reduce artificially the extended depth of field imposed on them by the diaphragm openings of the lenses used at the time. They employed gauze or plates of glass rubbed with Vaseline to that end, even using this latter trick to introduce areas of soft focus into a shot in which everything else at the same depth is sharply in focus (for instance the first scene in L'Herbier's *El Dorado* in which Eve Francis, sitting on a bench facing the camera in the middle of a row of girls, is quite noticeably in soft focus while her neighbors are in sharp focus). These film-makers were just as concerned with transitions from soft to sharp focus, which they attained chiefly by having their actors move in depth, an effect intensively explored by nearly every one of the great Russian directors, Eisenstein, Dovzhenko, Romm, and Boris Barnett in particular.

✳ In Japan, Ozu was equally intrigued by the possibilities of contrasts between soft and sharp focus, and *The Only Son* contains a series of shots that is astonishing in this respect. We first see two people seated facing each other, profiles toward the camera. A pillow in the foreground is in sharp focus while the characters in the background are in soft focus. As the conversation continues we see each of the two characters in turn full face in a shot and reverse shot, after which the camera returns to its initial angle. But now the pillow is in soft focus while the two people are seen sharply. This symmetrical structure, although an elementary and isolated example, already is evidence of a concern that we might describe as dialectical and that we come across in several other instances in this film and in others by Ozu. Evidences of this concern for the relationship between soft and sharp focus can be found in the work of many of the greatest contemporary film-makers as well, notably in that of Antonioni and Resnais, but chiefly in that of Bresson, where the two parameters are often strongly opposed, either for purely compositional reasons or, less frequently, for structural reasons, often in association with entrances and exits and an empty frame.

The other photographic parameters, at least in so far as black-and-white photography is concerned, have to do with actual light values, that is, with contrast and with tone, or brilliance, as it is called in television. A mixture of photographic styles systematically employed within a film, almost always in conjunction with an alternation in settings, between interiors and exteriors, as in Last Year at Marienbad (but also in numerous mass-audience films such as Divorce Italian Style), between past and present (as in Hiroshima mon amour), between dream and reality, summer and winter, and the like occurs fairly frequently. Another example is Joseph von Sternberg's first film, The Salvation Hunters, which is divided into three parts (exteriors, interiors, and exteriors, successively), each associated with an extremely characteristic photographic style. Such alternations (or gradations) in contrast and tone might conceivably be built up into autonomous structures, ones not necessarily occurring synchronously with changes in setting, thereby establishing a kind of complex dialectic within and between individual shots. It might be added that, even though this as yet may not have been done either in an all-black-and-white or an all-color film, it has nevertheless been undertaken in films involving a mixture of the two.[4] Experiments involving a mixture in the same film of black-and-white images and color images go back to the origins of film-making. The "primitives" (Méliès comes particularly to mind) sometimes tinted their films, either entirely or only in part. Abel Gance's masterpiece, *Napoleon*, went even further in this direction, as in the sequence in which Napoleon looks out over the sea from the top of a cliff, which introduces into a black-and-white context a series of shots all tinted differently, thus producing a remarkably striking visual effect. These experiments were more or less abandoned after the advent of color film,[5] but they have been taken up again in the last fifteen years by some of the younger film-makers. In *Night and Fog*, Resnais alternates color and black-and-white sequences; this depends, however, on yet another alternation, that between "documents from the past" and shots taken "in the present." Probably one of the first serious attempts at creating a structure centering around these two poles, a structure functioning independently of the narrative structure although dialectically related to it, is Monique Lepeuve's short film *Exemple Étretat*. This young film-maker has made several experimental films dealing with many fundamental problems of cinematic form and language, and, in this particular case, black-and-white images, monochromatic images in every tonality, and polychromatic images using every color in the spectrum as a dominant color or having no dominant color at all—in short, images exploiting every aspect of color taken in its largest sense—alternate in rapid succession. The editing of this film, moreover, sets up a complex underlying rhythm, another of whose elements is a mixture of live location shots and old picture postcards. One final element, a half-spoken, half-sung (and, on one occasion, whistled) commentary, which seems alternately to cleave to the images and draw apart from them, crowns the structure of a film that, brief and modest as it is, nevertheless represented an important step toward a much more complex use of film dialectics than the simple ones we have been discussing.

Before describing a third type of dialectic, we might linger for a moment on a particular type of contrast between color and black-

and-white, one that illustrates a procedure that has more general
applications and may in fact play a very important role in any
dialectical structure. This procedure consists of emphasizing one of
the two poles of a parameter by using it rarely or perhaps only
once, a concept that has rather striking analogies to a technique
used in post-Webernian serial music whereby a certain note or
register is emphasized. Rather than systematically alternating shots
or sequences in color and ones in black-and-white throughout a film,
certain film-makers have introduced a single sequence or even a single
shot in color into what is otherwise a purely black-and-white context (for example Agnès Varda in the precredit sequence of *Cleo
from Five to Seven* and Marcel Hanoun in the sequence at the race
track in *Le Huitième jour*). Doubtless the most startling use of this
technique is to be found in Kurosawa's *High and Low*, where a single pair of color shots unexpectedly appears on screen, ostensibly to
show a column of smoke whose color (red) is necessary as a plot
device, but in actual fact its very sudden, almost gratuitous, appearance is a striking signal marking the beginning of the third section
of the film, which is treated in a very different style from the two
preceding ones.

It is apparent, finally, that there exists a series of auditory parameters that correspond to these photographic parameters and that can
be (and often have been) organized into dialectical structures. However, these auditory parameters are so important that I prefer to
treat them in a separate chapter.

Let us now go on to the third classifiable type of dialectic (although
here my endeavor to be "encyclopedic" might well be questioned).
This third type might be called *organic dialectics*. The simplest of
these dialectics, obviously, is the opposition between an image and
its absence (which has as its corollary the opposition between the
presence and the absence of a sound track, as used throughout
Godard's *Deux ou trois choses que je sais d'elle*, for instance). We
are dealing here with a type of dialectical relationship that is different from those examined previously in that it is reduced to its two
poles; it is limited, that is to say, to a simple alternation (even
though a kind of subdialectic may be present within the pole constituted by the absence of an image, in the form of every possible
gradation in tone between a black screen and a white screen), for no

matter how illegible an image may be it still remains an image. The absence of an image on the screen traditionally constitutes a simple "punctuation mark" used to "signify" the passage of time in the same way a dissolve does. Academic film theoreticians have maintained that a dissolve suggests a shorter lapse of time than does a fade-out to black, a view that has no basis in perceptual reality and merely expresses a willful desire to attribute some inherent, organic value to a perfectly arbitrary convention. Film-makers such as Dovzhenko, Jean-Pierre Melville, and, above all, Bresson, while continuing to use the blacked-out screen as a punctuation mark, have nonetheless also sensed the possible structural value of the fade as compared to the essentially more plastic value of the dissolve. But it has been chiefly the young experimenters of the American "underground" cinema who have really endeavored to use the presence and absence of an image as poles equal in value, organizing whole films around this opposition. Stan Brakhage in *Reflections on Black* and Bruce Conner in *A Movie* both use long passages in which a dark screen plays a far more active role than that of a mere punctuation mark. But it is Ken Jacobs's *Blond Cobra* that I have principally in mind. Though a rather frivolous film in other respects, it includes very long sequences in which the screen remains completely black (as a result of a character having blocked the camera lens), while the voice of the inimitable Jack Smith tells one wild story after another. As the film unfolds, the "threat" of the black screen is felt more and more acutely each time a character approaches the camera (and the film-maker exploits this to the hilt, the film having been shot in some kind of garret and at "point-blank range"). It is this "threat" that ultimately provides this rather rudimentary dialectic with whatever interest it has.

We must now discuss two "triads" that on first reflection would seem to play a fundamental role in cinematic dialectics. The first of these involves backward motion and forward motion pivoting around the stationary image; the second consists of fast and slow motion centering around normal film velocity, with each of these two "triads" giving rise to two dialectical possibilities. Jean Epstein created a sort of aesthetic philosophy of film with these parameters as a foundation in his last theoretical writings, for he seems to have regarded them as the very cornerstone of film art. This bias caused him to put forward a number of ideas that strikingly foreshadow certain very contemporary concepts, especially those having to do with discontinuity, but in my view his theories are a bit too far removed from actual practice to be really relevant. Aside from their use as embellishments of the narrative (fast motion for "slapstick" effects, slow motion for "poetic" effect), there have been very few serious attempts to employ this series structurally, and even in these few instances fast or slow motion has had the conventional connotation. Only a few experimental films and Vertov's *Man with a Movie Camera* can be cited as examples of such an attempt. As a matter of fact, despite their deliberately spare and nonnarrative use in certain Kurosawa films, the effects that result from these parameters are too "expressionistic," too "magical" (rather like those created by distorting lenses) to function successfully independently of a narrative framework and can be approached structurally only on this narrative level.[6]

On the other hand, the opposition between the two poles constituted by the moving image and the stationary image has been used frequently for some years, sometimes in a more or less dialectical manner. Chris Marker made *La Jetée* entirely from stationary images (although this case in fact involves something else again—the use of photographs as a material, which will be discussed below), and the presence within that context of a single shot in which something actually moves (the girl opening her eyes) acts as the film's center of gravity. Truffaut in *Jules and Jim* and many of the younger English directors use the freeze frame as a kind of punctuation mark or as visual gags; the results are somewhat uneven.

Another organic dialectic, however, has proved to be relatively rich in possibilities: the opposition of live and animated shots. The probable inventor of this technique, Emile Cohl, was also the greatest pioneer of the animated film. His animated sequences were often bracketed by live sequences, but of principal interest here is the way in which he often introduced live figures into his brilliant cascades of graphic metamorphoses. In Walt Disney's hands, this principle became badly distorted, leading to such films as *Saludos Amigos*, in which the "realistic" relief and perspective of the animated sequences merely destroy the contrast effect so successfully employed by Cohl in his opposition of animated and live scenes. More recently, however, American and Czech animators have their similar techniques in a more modern and deliberately structural fashion. The outstanding example is Karl Zeman's masterpiece, *The Fabulous World of Jules Verne,* which contains an extremely varied mixture of the live and the animated throughout. In it Zeman used, perhaps for the first time, a medium shot of a live scene followed by a long shot of the same scene *manifestly* shot in animation (as against the "special effects" in *King Kong,* for example, which aim at creating an *illusory* continuity of materials). Zeman has continued to explore this mixture of live and animated actions in the features he has made since, but he has never equaled either the formal rigor or the poetic tension of this first film. This area nevertheless has a great many possibilities as yet unexplored, though Zeman's tendency to use a pastiche of graphic styles should be avoided if these are to lead anywhere.

Except for isolated examples such as Cohl's work, this concept of organic dialectics is relatively recent, unity of material and style having been an almost universally respected rule (inherited as it was from the traditional arts) until the advent of television. It might be added that this has been one of the greatest contributions made by the latter medium. By breaking down the barriers between genres and in particular by quite naturally introducing a mixture of the "live" and the "staged," television has encouraged the creation of new forms and new structures based on a deliberate mixing of genres and the materials inherent in them and has begun to explore the multiple dialectics that can result from such mixtures. In France, André S. Labarthe, the coproducer (with Janine Bazin) of the *Cinéastes de notre temps* series and its principal artistic director, is one of the film-makers to have best sensed these possibilities. In many of his programs (for example, on Gance, Godard, Roger Leenhardt) Labarthe attempts to structure the breaks in tone and style implicit in the alternate use of filmed interviews and other "raw" documents, on the one hand, and film-clips from the work of the film-maker in question, on the other, thus seeking to create a *discontinuous* essay form[7] to replace the often flat continuity of the classical documentary, an approach not unlike the discontinuous techniques of modern music. The program on Godard in particular employs a dialectic wherein obvious breaks in style and materials contrast with imperceptible "deferred" or "retroactive" transitions,

thus exploiting the ambiguous relationship between the mock-impro-
vised style of Godard's films and the straightforward interview style
(Godard converses with Labarthe in a car, while the streets seen in a
cutaway through the windshield are those of Godard's film *Alphaville*). Within cinema as opposed to television, it is Godard himself
who has most thoroughly explored melanges of styles and materials,
and a large number of his films have used these mixtures as an essential structural element. The extremely simple structure of *Vivre
sa vie*, consisting of separate sequences set off by titles (an original
mixture of materials in and of itself in a sound film), depends on
oppositions between the various styles of the sequences: real as versus
fake interviews, fake documentary style accompanied by voice-over,
fake newsreel footage, and so on. *Une Femme mariée*, which formally is a good deal less schematic, uses sudden (and numbered) inter-
jections of real (?) *cinéma-vérité* sequences into a staged context,
which in turn reaches at times a degree of abstraction that constitutes a third level of formal material; the film, moreover, is punctua-
ted throughout by the sudden appearance on screen of advertising
posters and slogans. The result of all this is a vast "time collage" in
which these stylistic breaks are intended to serve as an organizing
principle. The rhythm of the film is not entirely satisfactory, however, and the actors were perhaps not very well chosen for the dual
roles assigned them. This collage technique was later used more successfully by Godard in *Pierrot le fou*, where it became an integral
part of a more rigorous dramatic framework (which had its own
dialectic between "action" and "narration," to be examined in more
detail later). In this film, each sequence, though not strictly compart-
mentalized as in *Vivre sa vie* or *Une Femme mariée*, nonetheless
illuminates the central narrative framework in a number of quite
specific ways, generally through an explicit reference to a particular
genre (musical comedy, the gangster film, the television interview,
melodrama, the comic strip, the nightclub act, and so on). This alternation is thus not only an essential structural element in the film
but also one of its subjects.

Although Godard uses a whole range of relationships between the
camera and his characters, he very seldom films his actors without
their being aware of it. The only use of the candid-camera technique
with which I am acquainted in his work occurs in his second film,

Une Femme est une femme. As Susan Sontag has said, "It is not that Godard makes improvised films, it is just that he likes to give them the *look* of improvisation." Agnès Varda, on the other hand, has created in *Opéra-Mouffe* a unique example of a rigorously dialectical opposition between spontaneous "live" shots and "staged" shots, the link between the two types being provided by shots that are apparently spontaneous though actually planned beforehand. The strict compartmentalization of sequences, and above all the enormous range of differences in their relative durations, provides the essential framework around which the organization of this other dialectic hinges. The precise coloration that the dialectical relationship between the live and the staged assumes becomes all the richer because it extends over a range of expression reaching from "crude realism" (unrehearsed live images) to deliberately heightened, poetic "unreality" (planned images) with a rather delightfully ambiguous sort of *"fantastique social"* (apparently spontaneous but actually prearranged scenes) falling in between.[8]

Various attempts of this sort have since been made in featurelength films; Vilgot Sjöman's *I Am Curious* (*Yellow*) comes particularly to mind, constituting as it does a totally new dialectical reworking of the old gimmick of the film within a film. Certain techniques used in television programs (as discussed in Chapter 10) also come to mind.

Finally, although Godard successfully uses famous paintings as punctuating devices in his films, in much the same way[9] that he uses advertising posters, no other examples involving the satisfactory integration of painting into a dialectic of materials occurs to me. That, however, does not hold true for still photographs. William Klein in his *Float Like a Butterfly, Sting Like a Bee*, the anonymous editor of *October in Paris*, and, above all, the very talented Peter Emmanuel Goldman have all juxtaposed still photographs and live shots of the same scene in a rather striking way at times. In their work, transitions from one form of visual representation of an action to the other result in a very unusual sort of poetic and rhythmic vision.

The dialectics of film style begin at the level of individual shots and matches, as we have seen, although they may well result in structures underlying whole sequences and entire films. As for "photographic" dialects, they can function as easily between sequences as between shots. Of the "organic" dialects, some tend to function more between sequences—that is to say, they tend to follow a film's *narrative line*, as opposed to its *découpage* or plastic organization (were we to adopt the traditional distinction, which is rather incompatible with the views expressed here). Another extremely important type of dialectic must now be considered as well, one intimately connected with a film's narrative skeleton and therefore with the concept of a sequence, except in so far as certain contemporary filmmakers are endeavoring to make the individual shot as basic a narrative unit as the sequence. This is the dialectics of "narrative time," in other words the organization of the extended temporal jumps or ellipses, either forward or backward, dealt with in Chapter 1. It was apparently not until quite late in film history, notably with the flashbacks in Carné's *Le Jour se lève*, that the dialectical possibilities of narrative time were noticed. The articulation of flashbacks (or flashforwards) around an action unfolding in a film's "present tense" provides the most obvious means for structuring narrative time. But it is only recently that organic development of a simple linear progression in narrative time has been attained, by means of the complex dialectical structures that will constitute the subject of the next chapter.

The film best representing the contemporary attitude toward the flashback (its function, that is, in a nonchronological narrative that nonetheless refers to an implicit time-scale) is Jean-Marie Straub's *Nicht Versöhnt*. The history of modern Germany serves as the film's standard of temporal measurement, and its central dialectic is based on the manner in which sequences move forward or backward in time in relation to that standard. A completely different and infinitely more fertile approach is that used in *Marienbad*, whereby each sequence (or rather each sequence shot) refers to one or several other sequences in what is perhaps the past, perhaps the present, or perhaps a future "tense." This dialectic of ambiguity with its several variables[10] in itself engenders complex structures that are independent of the film's narrative structures (thematic variations on the statue, the woman at the balustrade, and so on) or its plastic values (the organization of camera movements, shot size, ellipses, and so on). The dialectics of time are too basic and involve too many other problems concerning the so-called form-content dichotomy for us to explore them in any greater depth within the limits imposed by this brief inventory of the principal simple dialectics. Whether one sets apart the dialectics of time as a separate series of relationships or whether they are included as part of the dialectical interactions between sequences, these latter in any event constitute a final major type of simple structure. These dialectical relationships between sequences are many and are a basic tool of film-makers.

Most screen writers, even the most commercially minded, know that it is best to create *some* kind of contrast between successive sequences, whether in duration, tempo, tone, or a combination of all three. Very few film-makers, however, attempt to structure their work in an *abstract* way by using these parameters. *Opéra-Mouffe* has already been cited in this chapter as a striking example of variations in the nature and duration of sequences, and in the first chapter we noted Fritz Lang's *M*. But the film-maker most concerned with problems of duration is undoubtedly Robert Bresson, particularly in his *Diary of a Country Priest* and subsequent films. Starting with predominantly short sequences, *Diary* progressively evolves to a point where long sequences predominate (the sequences, that is to say, do not actually last longer, longer sequences simply occur more frequently). The shorter sequences, moreover, are associated with a voice-over narration and with a supple, flowing rhythm, involving a great deal of compositional movement and reframing; the long sequences, on the other hand, are in synchronous sound and visually composed largely through the use of the shot and reverse shot technique. *The Trial of Joan of Arc*, by contrast, is much more regular in structure; what counts primarily here is the duration of successive shots as well as sequences, and even of the intervals separating the beginning or end of a line of dialogue from the beginning or end of a shot or sequence.[11] The film's entire underlying rhythm stems from these variations. In Bresson's films—so uniform in mood—conflicts and even variations in *tone* have little place. In current film practice these conflicts or variations in tone usually tend to resemble the alternation between melodrama and slapstick found in Renoir's *Diary of a Chambermaid*, a film from his American period, though usually the contrasts are not quite so jarring. A few years earlier, Renoir had very successfully exploited this parameter in *La Règle du jeu,* a beautifully orchestrated film famous precisely for its subtle mixture of tones and "genres."

Mr. Hulot's Holiday provides an even more important example. Here the contrast between sequences, simultaneously involving duration, tempo, tone, and setting (interiors or exteriors, night or day) is under constant, meticulous control, determining the whole progression of the film and constituting its principal source of beauty. Aside from the broken rhythm of the gags, so perverse and yet so perfect, the principal rhythmic factor is an alternation between strong and weak moments, between deliberately action-packed, screamingly funny passages and others just as deliberately empty, boring, and flat. When the pretty girl's companion shows her an absolutely empty seascape, visible from the window of her room, and says, "Sometimes people fish down there, but there's nobody there today," boredom is being put to good use. Similar scenes aimed at creating a feeling of real boredom go on for quite some time, but it is created in such carefully controlled "doses" that it plays a special rhythmic role in the film's over-all structure. There come to mind (among many other possible examples) the empty beach accompanied by the off-screen sounds of the restaurant dining room, the episodes of the child with his ice cream, the couple looking for seashells, etc.

In the whole history of cinema, this film, along with *Zéro de conduite,* has perhaps best succeeded in fulfilling the structural possibilities inherent in taking each sequence as a cellular unit, as an irreducible entity independent of any over-all spatial or temporal dialectic.

We have now only to mention a large number of other dialectics that are quite difficult to categorize: those concerning dialogue, the style of acting, the décor, make-up, and costumes—everything, in short, relating to the *explicit content* of images and sounds.

One of the most remarkable examples of a particular structure of this kind is to be found in Joseph von Sternberg's masterpiece, *The Blue Angel,* one of the greatest films in the history of cinema. In a certain sense, we are dealing here with the dialectics of sound, as the structure in question depends on whether the noise of what is happening out in the music hall is audible or inaudible during scenes occurring in the dressing rooms. The crucial strategy here is the use of a pair of doors constantly opening and closing in a marvelously complicated pattern; snatches of music, bursts of applause, and scraps of dialogue drift in as the doors are open and are cut off as they shut, each time in a different relation to the editing scheme. A structure of variations results that is exemplary in its rigor. Sometimes one of the doors (which one?—they all look alike and the space these dressing rooms define is one of the most totally abstract in cinema, analyzable only in terms of what each successive "composition" reveals) opens off screen, there is a sudden burst of music, followed by a shot of the door, which is then closed again. Sometimes a door opens on screen, the shot then shows something else, and it closes off screen. At times, the door opens or closes at the junction of two shots; at times, the door is opened or closed without affecting the ambient sounds—another unseen door perhaps has remained open. Jannings's return to "The Blue Angel" near the end of the film provides a kind of recapitulation of the structures employed in depicting his two previous visits to the nightclub. The very first scene in the classroom when Jannings opens the window, thereby allowing the "celestial" sound of the children's chorus to enter, is also a subtle prefiguration of this underlying pattern; moreover, it is the last time Jannings will be in control of events. The formal structure thus closely relates to the dramatic progression lying at the very heart of the film, Jannings's transition from an active to a passive role. (See also Chapter 9.)

The largest variety of structures of this sort is to be found in *Marienbad*, where they involve both lines of dialogue and dramatic incidents (either repeating them exactly, or with some variation, or recalling, alluding to, or prefiguring them) and décor (the progressive proliferation of furniture and ornamental motifs on the walls of the hotel room as well as its progressive increase in scale).

Yet another type of dialectic based on a film's décor occurs in one of Kon Ichikawa's most intriguing films, *The Actor's Revenge*, a work that employs a whole range of set styles, from a plain black background to totally realistic interiors, including painted backcloths and other essentially theatrical scenic devices between these two extremes. In a highly ambiguous sequence (halfway between dream and reality) a sort of thick, yellowish fog slowly clears to reveal the same fog painted on a theatrical backdrop. The film, moreover, uses theatrical conventions such as a *Doppelgänger* of the hero and the mixture of the comic and the tragic (devices possibly borrowed from Jacobean theater, consistently employed here in a thoroughgoing dialectical manner).

As for the style of acting, Alain Robbe-Grillet in *Trans-Europ-Express* performs an interesting experiment, juxtaposing scenes played by nonprofessionals and scenes played by professionals. This provides another structure, which is not yet fully developed here, and rather simplistically mirrors one aspect of the film's dramatic line, which itself is a bit simplistic. The film nevertheless is an indication that this structure may well develop into something quite complex, whereas the mixtures of amateur and professional actors that occur so frequently in Italian films have always been chaotic and seem to lead nowhere.

Robbe-Grillet's whole body of films (like several of his novels) employs structures evolving out of some form of itinerary or journey. His use in *Trans-Europ-Express* of the Paris-Antwerp run is dialectical, at least in our sense of the word used here, as is the double trajectory Michel Mitrani employs in his television film based on Samuel Beckett's *All That Fall*. In this latter film, the over-all schematic path of the action is first seen in a single shot taken from a helicopter, and that action is then played out in detail in the remainder of the film.

The task of defining the concept of structure or dialectics in general has been left until the end of this chapter, for its true nature is chiefly revealed through the multiplicity of forms it takes and its principal interest perhaps lies in the fact that it enables us to see how all kinds of investigations and experiments that might at first appear to be completely foreign to each other actually converge. It will be noticed that I have used the phrase "structure or dialectics." I have done so because I feel that in film the two concepts are more or less interchangeable, for structures almost always seem to occur in dialectical form—that is to say, a structure necessarily evolves within a parameter defined by one or more pairs of clearly delineated *poles*. Even a structure involving a progression or itinerary, although less simple internally perhaps, has two poles—a point of departure and a point of arrival (Paris and Antwerp in *Trans-Europ-Express*, for example). Generally speaking, then, a structure exists when a parameter evolves according to some principle of progression that is apparent to the viewer in the theater, or perhaps only to the film-maker at his editing table, for, even though there may be structures that are "perceptible only to those who have created them," they nonetheless play an important role in the final aesthetic result. Although the concealed forms present in *Wozzeck*, forms that Alban Berg hoped would always remain imperceptible to the listener, have often been enlisted to bolster up a certain philistine attitude, they nevertheless constitute a highly revealing precedent for film. As an art, film undoubtedly is closer to opera (at least opera as Berg conceived it) than it is to "pure" music, to which reference has perhaps been made too frequently.

It has recently occurred to me, moreover, that what we refer to as *structure* is perhaps no more than an extension of a concept that Russian and Anglo-Saxon film theoreticians continually dwelt on— namely, *rhythm*. Though I indicated at the beginning of this chapter that rhythm in film cannot be reduced to a succession of pure durations as is the case in music, I am tempted at this point to conclude that cinematic rhythm is defined by the sum total of all the parameters thus far enumerated and is therefore incredibly complex. For this precise reason, the temptation to reduce this enormous complexity to a simple analogy with music must be strictly avoided (and admittedly this has not always been done in the course of this discussion), if we are ever to grasp the essence of film form.

As should be obvious, and as a more thoroughgoing analysis would show, the structural principles noted thus far in a number of masterpieces are never applied in as systematic or as rigorous a manner as might seem to be the case from a general description such as that offered here. The rhythmic contrasts between the short and long sequences (and the accompanying contrast in styles of *découpage*) in Bresson's *Diary of a Country Priest* are certainly not of a mathematical rigor, and the film displays a large number of "deviations" from the norm established. Such deviations can themselves be built into even more elaborate formal patterns, though no example comes readily to mind except for my own unfinished film based on Georges Bataille's *Bleu du ciel*. Every sequence in this project followed what was perhaps an overly rigid principle of *découpage* (involving, for instance, a succession of shots and reverse shots in which the shot size progressively changed), which was violated at one or several key points in accord with another basic pattern that was itself a simple structure.

If we look back on this chapter, it may appear to be quite sketchy and schematic, for an enormous amount of ground had to be covered in a brief space. This reasonably complete inventory of simple structures nonetheless had to be drawn up before I could proceed to examine in greater detail a few of the complex dialectics that can result from them.

Notes

1. This, of course, is not the only cause of image illegibility: It can result from any form of visual interference such as reflections or fuzziness of image or a distracting element on the sound track—or even the width of the screen (as I indicate in my remarks on *Marienbad* below).

2. Markopoulos's great innovation consists in his alternation of unbearably prolonged shots and one-frame flashes, and even more importantly in his insertion during the most beautiful moments in films such as *Twice a Man* and *Himself as Herself* of one-frame close-ups, these close-ups consisting of details from the larger composition into which they are inserted. This technique has a good many possibilities, but it has not as yet been developed in the manner that it deserves.

3. Valerian Borowczyk's masterpiece, *Goto, l'île d'amour*, for the time being represents the ultimate application of this notion and is also a fine instance of the use of a "complex dialectic" (such as will be discussed in the following chapter).

4. It is obvious that breaks and contrasts in style have been attempted in a much freer way in color films than they have ever been in black-and-white (as in Antonioni's *Red Desert* and Resnais's *Muriel*).

5. Alternations between color and black-and-white sequences for purely narrative purposes (as in *Stairway to Heaven* or *Bonjour Tristesse*) have been disregarded.

6. André Hodeir, however, has proposed a rather fascinating use for reverse motion. A sequence might be shown with all the images in normal forward motion and then be repeated with the images in reverse motion (with perhaps a different sound track as well), with the series of images in each case having a perfectly understandable though completely different meaning.

7. See Chapter 10.

8. We should not overlook the greatest pioneer in this area, Dziga Vertov, who juxtaposes "live" images with "staged" ones in a surprisingly modern way in his *Man with a Movie Camera*.

9. *Formally* the same, that is. It should be made clear that, when referring to a

parameter's structural function, I am not overlooking the fact that the parameter performs other functions as well within the complex object that a film represents.

10. One that Jean Epstein had advocated and experimented with as early as 1927 in *La Glace à trois faces*, his first film to embody his belief that "there are no stories, there never have been any stories, there are only events with neither head nor tail, with neither beginning nor end."

11. This particular parameter has an obvious corollary involving the length of time that elapses between a movement into or out of frame and a shot change. These intervals, as we have seen, play a very important role in Bresson's work.

5

Absence of Dialectic
and Complex Dialectics

The preceding chapter drew up a kind of inventory of the many simple dialectics that may be detected in the formal strategies of a given film. Before going on to examine some examples of the complex structures that can result from the more or less deliberate and carefully planned combination of several simple structures, a long parenthesis is in order. At least one of the conclusions that can be drawn from the brief analysis in the preceding chapter is that any film contains dialectical structures, if only because there is bound to be some degree of contrast between sequences (however unpronounced) and some sort of interaction between the shot changes within a given sequence (however banal). This is not to say that there are more than a handful of films in which these "dialectics" are used in any systematic way, and films in which there is any real organic coordination between them are even rarer. In most cases, these dialectics merely exist in what might be termed their crude natural state, as simple unorganized alternations. These alternations nevertheless are embryonic structures, so to speak, and the fact that they exist is welcome confirmation that the ideas set forth in this book, and above all the hopes expressed for future developments in cinema, are not mere speculation but, rather, conclusions that can be drawn from *current film practice.*

On a number of occasions in the history of cinema, there have been attempts to abolish all formal dialectics at the level of *découpage* and use only what I might call a "dialectic of images." Many of these experiments have been very interesting; one of the most recent of them, Jean-Daniel Pollet's *Méditerranée,*[1] is also one of the most radical, for it is a film with no "matches" whatsoever. It consists, in other words, of juxtaposed recurrent shots that have no connection between them other than their relationship (with one exception) to the *mare nostrum*—statues, landscapes, still-lifes . . . as well as a similarly recurring shot of a girl on an operating table —the film-maker hoping that the order in which the individual shots follow one another on the screen will awaken some kind of poetic echo or resonance in the viewer's mind that will somehow evoke the ineffable feelings, the *je ne sais quoi* that he himself doubtless experienced while viewing these same juxtapositions of images. This approach bears a certain resemblance to the "montage of attractions" advocated by the young Eisenstein, a conception of editing that, it might be added, the Russian master subsequently repudiated once he realized that film form essentially depends on a dialectical opposition between a continuity and a discontinuity. There are indeed elements of a dialectic in *Méditerranée.* A spoken commentary and a musical score accompany this series of unfolding images. However, just as the juxtaposition of images obeys a kind of total empiricism, a blind faith that *something* will always result, so the relationship between images and commentary is completely arbitrary, as if the film-maker had been content to let commentary and images develop independently, confident that they would "go well together." This is not to say that secret affinities between the images and the commentary do not exist, for undoubtedly they do. And surely we should not deprecate a film simply because it is "obscure." Film has long since gone past the stage where simple narrative statements are sufficient. Nonetheless, if the space-time of both commentary and images is to be something more than the mere setting of two continuities seemingly blissfully unaware of each other's existence side by side with no dialectical or any other kind of structure being thereby created, their actual meeting points, the moments at which the two continuities converge, must not be completely fortuitous (film form having also gone beyond the Surrealist aesthetic that found transcendent meaning in such events as the "chance encounter of a sewing machine and an umbrella on a dissecting table"), and the relationship between image and commentary must not be indecipherable, for obscurity of meaning does not necessarily imply an "illegible" structure. In fact, it may even be maintained that the more hidden the meaning of a work is, the more apparent the principles of structural tension underlying it should be. The main element absent in *Méditerranée* is precisely that *tension*, without which no work of art will seem to be a deliberate creation rather than pure happenstance.

What is missing, in short, is an *organized interaction:* Only the *encounter* between the separate formal elements appears to have been planned, for the actual *forms* of this encounter seem gratuitous. A rather deliberate attempt at structuring this succession of shots had admittedly been made, for they are very few in number and have been constantly repeated for *different durations* of time. Whether concerted or not, this may represent something of an attempt to apply principles similar to those of serial music, whereby the entire work is based on the constant permutations of a very small number of formal objects (a series or tone row of twelve tones in different registers, a certain group of intervals, a certain range of tone qualities, and so on), these permutations bearing principally on the order of occurrence and on the relative duration of these various elements.

I must, however, insist once again on the limits inherent in an imitative approach of this sort. A musical tone is a basic element and there are only twelve of them, or so the chromatic approach to serial music would have it. The restricted nature of the basic musical material in twelve-tone compositions is therefore an organic fact. To limit the range of basic film material in a similar way is a very arbitrary decision in my view. Moreover, each musical tone is unique; therefore, when tones are combined into a new formal entity, the result is something a good deal more autonomous relative to the initial components than is the case when two rather haphazardly chosen shots are spliced together. Two successive sounds always have a *vertical* relationship, since the ear situates them on a chromatic scale, as well as a *horizontal* relationship in time, this twofold relationship constituting only one of many dialectical dimensions of musical discourse. Musical parameters are so tightly interwoven that even very simple material can yield extremely rich developments, whereas, in film, limiting the material necessarily limits what can result. The images in *Méditerranée* are linked only horizontally in time. They are more or less long, more or less short, and reappear with this or that frequency. But there is no vertical link between them, since they have been purposely chosen because of their mere disparity. Those vertical relationships between shots provided in part in cinema by the forms of spatial and temporal articulations and by plastic relationships created through editing are entirely absent here. The lack of tension, the feeling of monotony, we experience watching *Méditerranée* unfold—despite the beauty of certain shots, of the narration, and even of the music, in and of themselves—stems from this fact.

It might seem rather strange to have lingered for so long on a film that seems to have taken the wrong track. This mistaken approach teaches us an important lesson, however. Film form,[2] it would appear, simply cannot exist without some kind of underlying dialectic; the mere linear alternation of disparate images does not suffice to create a film. Interestingly enough, Pollet's subsequent film, *Le Horla*, based on the Maupassant tale, seemed to evince the maker's awareness of this fact, at the same time as it was a development of the discontinuity principle of *Méditerranée*.

Le Horla is also based on using a minimum amount of material, repeating shots for constantly varying durations, but here the play of permutations operates in conjunction with another simultaneously unfolding continuity, a voice-over narration that establishes a sort of standard of temporal measurement. Each image can be situated more or less precisely relative to the time established by the narration, and the viewer is thus aware of jumps in time and space. These transitions almost automatically create tensions and rhythms that link the film's separate components together in a single formal structure. When repeated a second time, the shot of someone walking down a corridor strikes the viewer as both the "same" shot as before and a "new" shot, because it now occupies a different position in narrative time. In *Méditerranée*, by contrast, the voice-over established no temporal structure of its own, and therefore it seems to the viewer that he is merely seeing the same shot over and over, *ad nauseam*, and variations in the duration of shots seem to be a mere intellectual exercise on the part of the film-maker. In other words, the repetitions of shots in *Le Horla* move the film forward and strengthen its unity, whereas in *Méditerranée* they cause the film simply to mark time or to fall into meaningless bits and snippets. This does not mean that only a conventional narrative can provide a valid framework. In *Le Horla*, the contrast between the old-fashioned style of narration (Maupassant's text) and the daring with which it is visually developed is in fact quite disconcerting. One can very easily conceive of other possible forms of relationship between an image and a verbal text, but these must necessarily be *temporal*. The important point to be made about *Le Horla* is that the relationship established between the various elements is structural and organic. The film's component elements are not simply set side by side and end to end in the mistaken belief that the juxtaposition of several "beautiful" elements will always be more beautiful than any one of them taken separately, which seems to us to be the notion underlying *Méditerranée*.

This radical disjunction of word and image constitutes a dialectical principle often followed in film. In *Rope*, Hitchcock makes use of it to create a particularly tense feeling of suspense as the camera lingers for long moments on a housemaid methodically clearing the top of the chest in which the dead body has been hidden; at the same time, a long voice-off conversation, very relevant to the drama at hand, but completely unrelated to the visual image, is taking place between several of the characters.

The sequence in the Institute of Semantics in Godard's *Alphaville* unfolds according to similar principles, and the complexity and the pronounced dissimilarity between the two component elements (Alpha's speech off screen and the flashlights darting around in the dark) is such that the film must be seen several times before the scene can be grasped in its entirety. Jerzy Skolimowski uses this same technique much more systematically, and his first two films are based almost entirely on the pronounced sense of disorientation that results from this sort of radical disjunction. Another film, however,

Michelangelo Antonioni's *Cronaca di un amore*, the whole structure of which hinges on a similar dissociation of sound and image, represents an almost unparalleled achievement, an accomplishment so successful that this masterpiece should be considered a perfect example of its kind and analyzed in detail.

The film is proof of a firm bias (in the nobler sense of that word) in favor of stripping the image of any sort of narrative function. From the point of view of "story-telling," *practically nothing ever occurs on the screen*. But, even though *Cronaca di un amore* is not exactly an "action film," neither is it a film that "has no plot," for the narrative line deals with two violent deaths (one a murder by "omission"), machinations aimed at a second murder, and an investigation by a private detective. Clara and Guido cause the death of Guido's fiancée, an obstacle to their love, by doing nothing to prevent her from falling down an elevator shaft. However, her demise causes the two lovers to have a falling-out. A few years later a wealthy Milanese industrialist whom Clara has married solely for his money begins to brood about his wife's past, and has a private detective agency investigate it. This investigation indirectly results in the reunion of the two lovers; their love is rekindled, and they soon get around to plotting the husband's death. The detective learns that they have become lovers again and informs the husband. Stunned by this revelation, the husband proceeds to kill himself at the wheel of his car just a few miles before he reaches the bridge where Guido is lying in wait to murder him. Once again a death that the two lovers have ardently wished for, but that they cannot be accused of causing, separates them.

This narrative symmetry could easily have resulted in a coincidence-packed melodrama of the worst Hollywood sort (as the pastiche Bardem made on the same subject amply proves). Antonioni, however, has constructed one of the most perfectly and completely structured films in the entire history of cinema out of this narrative material, essentially through the disjunction of spoken word and image that we have referred to.

During the golden age of film theater (the 1930's), films in which the essential action occurred in verbal rather than visual form, films that would be totally incomprehensible were the sound to be turned off, were naturally quite common. The pendulum had simply swung

back, so to speak, for during the heyday of the silent film the ultimate aim had been to create essentially a *visual* narrative line, reducing the number of interposed titles to a strict minimum. The talkies
of the 1930's—and how talkative they were!—were based on love
stories and comedies of manners, narrative material well suited to
this form of filmed commercial theater, and the entire action could
very easily be staged within a single bedroom or living room, for the
spoken word was the action. The microphone and to a meager extent
the camera (for, if the visuals were completely eliminated, the film
would still be quite understandable) were above all *narrative* tools
(the remarks on "the zero point of cinematic style" in Chapter 1
being quite relevant here).

In *Cronaca di un amore*, however, something altogether different
occurs. The spoken word is no longer the action. Rather, it is a narrative vehicle that *describes* all of the action that has already occurred or will (perhaps) occur. One of the film's basic structures, in
fact, consists of the dialectical interaction between the spoken descriptions unfolding on the screen and the past or future actions to
which they refer.

Thus, as the film begins, the head of the detective agency *tells*
one of his investigators about the husband's suspicions; several wit-
nesses *tell* the detective about Clara's childhood and adolescence; an
old friend of the lovers *tells* Guido (by letter) about the detective's
visit to her; Guido *tells* Clara what their friend has told him, and so
on. *Cronaca di un amore* thus essentially consists of a long series of
recounted facts and intentions expressed verbally, and the rare sequences, usually arguments or love scenes, in which the spoken word
becomes genuine action, as in yesterday's film theater, constitute
exceptional poles in the film.

Whether the spoken word is a narrative vehicle or the basic action,
the result in either case is that the *complete freedom of the camera
is restored*. Rather than attempting to reproduce theatrical space, as
the American directors of the 1930's endeavored to do, or performing
perfectly gratuitous arabesques around an otherwise absolutely banal
theatricality, as Aldrich does in *The Big Knife*, Antonioni creates a
relationship between his characters as they speak and his camera as it
records them speaking, which can perhaps best be described as a
ballet. It is a ballet, moreover, of an unprecedented complexity and

rigor. In Chapter 2, we have already seen how the space defined by the very prolonged shots of this film is organized internally through movements into and out of frame, how fluctuations in the suggested extent of off-screen space are determined by off-screen glances, and so on. What is particularly important to emphasize at this point, however, is that in *Cronaca di un amore* the camera movement neither humbly follows the "natural" movements of the actors, as in academically transparent cinema, nor weaves the arbitrary and frenetic arabesques around the actors' movements characteristic of the films of a Max Ophuls or an Alexandre Astruc. Rather, the manner in which both the camera and the actors move is equally stylized, with each of these two sets of movements determining the possibilities of the other. Thus the similarity to a ballet: The camera at every moment executes something equivalent to a dance step, with not only the actors as partners in the choreography but the shadows they cast as well. Di Venanzo's admirable lighting and Piero di Filipone's sets are in fact set up in such a way that there is only a single, relatively dark shadow for each actor, the image contrast otherwise remaining quite low. Of course, the ballet is not so much between the camera and the actors as between the actors and the evolving spatial area as defined by the camera: the field, or rather its two-dimensional projection, the frame. The dynamic progression of this ballet depends on constant changes in image composition through the use of every conceivable technique, by reframing, by having extras move through frame, and above all by movements into and out of frame and by changes in shot size within the shot. This constant recomposition of the film's space is its essential plastic characteristic.

Another important element in the film's underlying rhythm is the continual alternation between short (usually single-shot) sequences making maximum use of off-screen space (as when the detective is in the newspaper office or when he meets with his colleague in the police force) and longer sequences, involving two or three shots (the sequence in the night club, the film's key scene, being singularly privileged in that it extends over some ten or more shots). The film's only weakness lies in the manner in which the shot changes function. Because of the length of many of the shots, the fact that cuts from one shot to the next are disruptive breaks is very obvious

and consequently they should logically have some extremely important function to fulfill. In actual fact, however, the transitions are
often quite awkward and serve no purpose. One often feels that cuts
occur simply because the director has run out of dolly tracks—or of
imagination. The fact that there are almost no abridgements within
sequences, except for those of a very banal sort (such as transitions
from interiors to exteriors), is especially noticeable. It is an understandable approach, but one that makes striking cuts perhaps much
harder to come by. There are, however, a few remarkably successful
shot changes, due nearly every time to some break in spatial continuity. In the first of two hotel rooms where the lovers meet, a very
prolonged shot during which, among other things, Clara looks for a
misplaced earring is followed by an empty frame showing a corner
of the bed. Clara then crawls into frame to pick up the earring that
Guido has just thrown on the bed; this justification for the shot is
not provided, however, until several seconds after the transition has
occurred, thereby making the break in spatial continuity all the more
emphatic. In a later scene during which the lovers take refuge on a
staircase, we follow their ascent in a series of long crane shots, and,
just as we hear the loud off-screen sound of an elevator door slam-
ming shut, the lovers break off their argument (they are already talking about murdering the husband) and lean over the railing, sharing
the same painful memory of Guido's fiancée falling to her death
down the elevator shaft. The next shot shows the elevator approaching the camera from a very pronounced downward angle. The shot is
invariably experienced by the viewer as a "subjective" shot, as something the lovers see. Nevertheless, when a tilt, begun as the elevator
started upward, brings the camera back to a horizontal position, we
realize that it is actually on the other side of the elevator shaft, and
that the lovers still looking over the railing are actually facing us and
quite a distance away. In both cases, a "retroactive" match of the
kind described in the first chapter is involved, a technique that I feel
is one of the many possible ways in which a shot change can be
brought forcibly to our attention and its essential nature as a break
revealed, a fact of which Antonioni, in spite of my criticism, is a
good deal more aware than most film-makers.[3]
    This scene also brings us face to face with an essential problem in-
herent in any view of film form as a dialectical interaction: Because

of this radical disjunction between images (here treated as an almost abstract ballet) and spoken words (here treated as the sole narrative vehicle), how can the two components be interrelated?

To have maintained this separation between sound and image throughout, shooting each sequence with this disjunction alone in mind (with an image ballet on the one hand and a word narrative on the other, as is the case in the admirable sequence in the empty regatta basin), would have been to reject the possibility of an essential structural unity in the form of a continual and alternating series of divergences and convergences between sound and image, a dialectical rhythm that sometimes joins and sometimes separates what used to be called form and content. The transition between shots in the elevator shaft as described above provides an example of how this dialectical interaction functions. We are visually reminded of the lovers' thoughts and words for the few seconds during which the shot appears to be subjective (even though such subjective shots are extremely rare in this film). The moment we realize our "mistake," we are once again "outside" the characters' minds, and image and word move apart again. The great number of ways in which narrative and image are related in *Cronaca* is remarkable. (The "symbolic" method just alluded to occurs only once.) When the maid, present during the fatal elevator accident, recounts her version of the death scene, only on one occasion do her present actions coincide with her past actions: Having gone off to put her shopping basket away, she then runs back to the landing where the detective awaits her, simultaneously recounting how she had run toward the elevator after her young mistress had fallen down the shaft. (There is a similar device in *"Tentato suicidio,"* the sketch Antonioni contributed to the group film *Amore in città.*) The violence below the surface erupts on screen only four times: when Guido slaps Clara at the nightclub, at their first tryst in a cheap hotel room, on the bridge, and when Clara pretends to strangle Guido in a second hotel-room scene. These four moments are key points in the film as well. The accident in which the husband dies occurs as a very distant sound followed by a tiny glimmer of light on the horizon. Because of its marvelous understatement, this device permits Antonioni to respect the essential principle underlying the entire film (the elimination of all on-screen action), and at the same time it fulfills the need to highlight this particular moment by "showing" it rather than recounting it. A few shots later, the only "realistic" (in the sense of "repugnant") image in the film occurs, the one occasion on which Antonioni violates his principle of extreme and elegant stylization, and also a particularly dramatic moment of convergence between story and image: a close-up of the husband's dead body.

In the films Antonioni has made subsequently (*Cronaca di un amore* was his first feature-length work), he has unfortunately been excessively preoccupied with problems of content and, with the exception of *La Notte* and *L'Éclisse*, has dealt only incidentally with structural problems. He is obviously extremely conscious of these latter, but at the same time he seems wary, and even suspicious, of them. In *Cronaca di un amore*, however, he attempted to deal with a whole range of basic problems, ones that should be of utmost concern to every contemporary film-maker, and even if he was not able to solve all of them, the film represents an absolute turning point in the history of cinema.

*   *   *

Although little attention was paid it for a number of years, *Cronaca di un amore* is almost universally hailed as a masterpiece today, while another work that seems to me to be the second turning point in the history of cinema in the last twenty years remains almost entirely unknown to film-lovers and even to most young film critics.

Marcel Hanoun's *Une Simple histoire* was coproduced by the French national television network and the director in 1958–59. The film was shot in 16 mm on a very low budget. Hanoun quite literally made the film all by himself. *Une Simple histoire* nonetheless is as far removed as possible from the kind of improvised reportage that might reasonably have been expected considering the shooting conditions and subject of the film. The "plot," inspired by an item on the back page of a newspaper, has a bare, spare pathos reminiscent of one of Cesare Zavattini's classic film synopses: A woman, in all likelihood an unwed mother, arrives in Paris with her child, a little girl six or seven years old. She has only a hundred francs in her purse and has come to the city to look for work. Although she is taken in at first by a friend who lives on the outskirts of the city, she is soon forced to move from one dreary hotel to another, when her friend, fearing that the woman's presence in her house may inconvenience her lover, asks her to leave. A futile search for work follows, and she also has difficulty finding a room or keeping one more than a few days because she has a child, a hard time finding someone to care for her little girl while she looks for a job, and many other vicissitudes. Finally, after a certain number of days have gone by, her money is all gone, and she and the child are forced to spend the night in a vacant lot but are taken in the next morning by a kind woman who lives in a low-income housing project across the street. Such is the story, indeed a very simple one. Yet, starting from this basic skeleton, Hanoun constructs the most elaborate, most rigorously controlled formal structure of any feature film thus far made. In my opinion, Hanoun has created one of the few genuine masterpieces in the entire history of cinema.

The narrative line, as briefly described above, actually pivots around a single very important break, in the form of a flashback, which occurs some ten minutes into the film. At the beginning of the film the kind lady looks out of her window, sees that a woman and child have spent the night outdoors, and goes down to take them in. Later, alone in the lady's apartment with the little girl, Sylvie, the woman recalls everything that has happened to her since she has come to Paris. From that moment on the story is such as I have described it, right up until the night spent in the vacant lot. In addition, however, the film closes in a remarkable and strikingly original way: The circle is never fully completed, for we never return to the present; the flashback is left open, so to speak.

The entire film, including all the action prior to the flashback, is accompanied (although, as we shall see, "accompanied" is much too weak a term) by an off-screen commentary, spoken by the woman, which constitutes the basic structural feature of the film. To an inattentive viewer, the woman's running commentary appears to be merely redundant, and, during the film's brief run in two Paris art houses, her off-screen narration was greeted by continuous howls of laughter on the part of the audience. This is simply because it nearly always violates a cardinal rule, one discussed in any elementary manual on "how to make a perfect film": It describes what is on the screen before the viewer and repeats what has already been said in "synchronous" sound (an admittedly inaccurate term as the film was of course entirely post-synchronized). But if this is all the viewer sees in the commentary he is indeed inattentive, for anyone who pays closer attention soon notices that it functions in an altogether different manner, that its relationship to both the visual images and the spoken dialogue is constantly shifting in an extraordinary and extremely complex way throughout the entire film, in accord with a principle of variation fully deserving the term *dialectical*, which has been used perhaps a bit too loosely elsewhere in these pages. I shall now endeavor to define the poles between which the parameters of this commentary evolve.

First of all, with only two notable exceptions, the commentary functions as a simple statement of fact. The woman describes what is happening to her, what she has seen or what she has been told (even mentioning the fact that there have been times when she has said nothing or been told nothing), or (much less frequently) what she has thought or felt. On only one occasion do her remarks take the form of a complaint or rebelliousness, and even in this case they are presented as if they were just another statement of fact. Toward the end of the film, unable to sleep, she discovers in a drawer in her hotel room a magazine of the *True Confessions* variety with the story told in photos, and describes its contents (off screen) in more or less the following words: "Everyone in it was very good-looking, they drove sports cars, they didn't have to work, and drank whisky all day long." This provides a first example of Hanoun's amazing sense of a "privileged moment," with another occurring on the one occasion when the woman refers to what her life was like prior to the tribulations she is now undergoing: "I thought of going back to Lille; my father might have taken me back, but my stepmother would have made it rough for me."

Let us now examine the structural relationships between the commentary and the spoken dialogue. As it endlessly repeats what has already been said, the commentary alternates between a direct and an indirect style of narration, either quoting words already spoken on screen with the quotation marks understood or simply summarizing what has previously been said. Whenever there is an actual quotation, it is at times perfectly accurate and at other times inaccurate, whether because of inversions, substitutions of one word for another, or omissions of certain words, or a mixture of these. When a summary occurs, it may contain a quotation (either exact or inexact) or be simply a précis of the previous dialogue that may or may not be accurate, for the order of ideas expressed may be changed or there may be omissions. What gives this interaction its relief, however, is the varying time intervals between the off-screen commentary and the actual on-screen dialogue. The voice-over can completely precede the phrase spoken on screen or completely follow it (and at relatively longer or shorter intervals as well, naturally), these two possibilities constituting the outer limit of a vast range of overlappings between narration and dialogue, going so far as to include their exact congruence, when a phrase of dialogue and a phrase of the narration are precisely equal in length, although not necessarily identical in wording. Consequently it very often happens that the meaning of a given phrase can be grasped only by listening to both of the overlapping tracks simultaneously, key words emerging out of the more jumbled, incomprehensible portions to complete the meaning of what was heard during other more clearly understandable portions. I believe I am safe in saying that the same "pattern" of the two elements never recurs, for on no occasion are the disparities in time and wording exactly similar, and the "reading" of each new group is thus a different adventure. At times a phrase starts simultaneously on both tracks but ends on two different words or at two different points in time; conversely, the two tracks may start out of phase and end on the same word or at the same time. When to these many variables, we add the range of relationships between sound levels that Hanoun has created in the sound mix, extending from a perfect balance of the volume of the two tracks to the total suppression of the "synchronous" spoken words, we have some small idea of the vast realm of possibilities open to Hanoun, and he has resolutely attempted to exhaustively exploit them.

As I have already said, the commentary not only describes the words and gestures of individual characters and the objective facts but also allows the woman to express her thoughts and feelings. In this case, however, what may be described as a "structuring by elimination" comes into play, an altogether remarkable device both because of its formal and its poetic effect.[4] As the woman's situation worsens, she increasingly shrinks from revealing her thoughts or her feelings (having shown these latter only three or four times previ-

ously anyway). Her voice-over remarks become flatter and more
dully matter-of-fact and even include a line whose overwhelming
banality indicates how severe the alienation this woman is undergoing is and thus constitutes the crowning moment of the film. As
she stops near a railing on one of the city's outer boulevards, she
says in voice-over: "I walked by an underpass. Cars were going in one
end and coming out the other." The scene in the vacant lot follows,
a sort of pathetic coda during which we hear her "inner monologue" again, very briefly: "And then I no longer remember . . . I
found myself in a vacant lot . . . I bundled Sylvie up in my raincoat
. . . she fell asleep . . . I did too . . . I woke up with a start . . .
I was afraid . . . I was cold [a very long close-up of the woman
staring off into space follows, and then a long shot of the housing
development, the final image in the film] . . . lights were still on in
some of the windows."

Successfully describing the dialectical interaction between commentary and image in *Une Simple histoire* involves examining both
the film's visual structure and its temporal dialectics. A close reading
of the scenario would no doubt allow us to determine how many days
pass between the woman's arrival in Paris and the morning when she
is taken in by the charitable lady. The passage of narrative time,
however, is not made "palpable" through the actual succession of
days and nights on the screen, but rather through the way in which
the woman's hundred francs dwindle away, for she is shown again
and again anxiously counting and recounting her money. Using this
concrete device to make us acutely aware of the passage of time,
Hanoun's *découpage* employs throughout an amazing variety of temporal ellipses within the time flow thus established. Regardless of
whether or not it preserves spatial continuity, a shot transition can
abridge any amount of time ranging from a few seconds to twenty-
four hours or more. Hanoun is the first modern film-maker to my
knowledge to have systematically abridged time through changes of
scale along the same camera angle.[5] So as to make the constant
variations in the extent of time abridged both apparent and *aesthetically functional*, Hanoun naturally incorporates the voice-over
commentary into his system of ellipses. The simple indication of the
actual extent of time abridged is not all that is involved (although
that too sometimes occurs, as when an admirable match along one

camera angle indicates the passage of a whole night through a very minor change between the scales of two successive close-ups, each showing the woman in bed but each lit differently, with the second of these followed by the woman saying: "I woke up in the morning. It was the overly bright sun that woke me . . ."). Hanoun uses the voice-over mainly to create some sense of what transpires in the time span abridged in these very abrupt elisions (there is not a single dissolve in the film and very few fades). At one point, a shot taken in the hotel room is followed by a long shot out in the street. The woman is shown holding her child by the hand and bending down to pick up a croissant lying on the sidewalk, as the commentary says: "I bought a croissant for Sylvie . . . she didn't want it and threw it away . . ." Yet, before the sentence ends, she has offered the croissant to a bum who staggers by. And the remaining portion of the scene is recounted with a very noticeable lag not only between verbal text and visual image but also between the moment when we grasp what is going on and the moment when the woman describes the scene in the voice-over, one of many forms of possible interaction between narration and image. The woman never uses the word "bum": He is, in her words, a "man" passing by, and only at the very end of the scene does she rather delicately add that "he had been drinking" although from the moment he appeared on the screen it has been obvious to the viewer that he is dead drunk.

Another scene provides some indication of how complex the interaction between the forms of temporal contraction and the voice-over can become. Having seen an ad in the paper with the address of a company that is hiring people, the woman and child make their way down to the *Métro*. In the next shot, the woman walks past a street sign, exits, and the screen remains empty. The voice-over says, "I finally found the street." An establishing shot of the inside of a café follows. Sylvie is seated in the foreground with her back to the camera, and the voice-over continues, "I had asked someone to take care of Sylvie, but even so the job had been taken by the time I got there." At this point, the woman walks into frame and sits down facing Sylvie and the camera. In a matching medium shot from the same camera angle, the woman lifts her head and looks toward the camera. "I ordered a cup of chocolate," the commentary continues. There then follows a new shot, still from the same angle, as she drinks her chocolate in close-up. "Sylvie had gone outside without my noticing [she lifts her head toward the camera], but the waitress saw her and brought her back inside." A new shot from the same angle takes us back to the initial composition. Sylvie is once again (or still?) sitting facing her mother with the waitress already exiting from frame. In this extremely complicated scene, the narration not only suggests the action taking place in the span of time omitted between shots (resulting in this case in the complete elimination of all dialogue in the scene, all the supposed lines having been spoken in the intervals between shots) but also suggests events taking place in a kind of no-man's land, for they might be construed as occurring either off screen or during some portion of abridged time. *Une Simple histoire* abounds in complex structures of this sort, never before used by any film-maker.

Other more "incidental" structures, finally, are grafted onto these overarching dialectical movements, which play the primary role in determining the film's formal structure as a whole. These incidental structures are based on the woman's various encounters, such as her different confrontations with hotel-keepers and others (though we never actually see the people she asks for jobs). The most interesting of these structures appears to me to be the one centered on her search for food. On five separate occasions, the voice-over speaks of the purchase of either milk or some kind of canned goods, yet we never witness the actual buying or consuming of any of these items, only their preparation on a gas burner in hotel rooms. This preparation of food, which becomes one of the obsessive themes in the film, is prefigured before the flashback by a very brief dream the woman has as she dozes off in her chair in the lady's apartment: A gas burner sits in the middle of a vacant lot and the woman dances happily around it heating up some milk as the birds sing and the sun shines brightly. On the last day, however, just before the woman vacates her last hotel room, we finally witness the purchase and consumption, though not the actual preparation, of food. This constitutes a kind of "negative reversal" of the structure as so often repeated previously. The formally crucial moment this reversal in structure represents is followed by a similar one. While buying a croissant for Sylvie (the third one to appear in the film, the first having been given to the child by a kind-hearted waitress), the woman does something foolish with the little money she has left—she buys her daughter a little surprise-package, resulting in the only line in the entire film spoken by Sylvie. "It's ugly," she says, as she throws away the favor she found in the paper cornucopia.

Besides these patterns with variations repeated all through the film, there are a number of formal devices that occur only very rarely, but that are structurally linked through their complete "unreality" in an otherwise "realistic" context. The dream described above is the first example. A day spent searching for work is depicted by a long single close-up of the woman looking into the camera, raising and lowering her eyes as a montage of factory noises indicates the compression of time. In the shot immediately following, another "magical" device occurs, in the form of another temporal ellipsis. The woman exits from a building and then from frame, leaving the screen empty, as the voice-over says that at one place they told her to return the next day. She then exits from the building and from frame once again with no intervening change of shot. "But the next day there was nothing," the commentary says. (The fact that two "magical" devices are used in immediate succession in itself constitutes a form of emphasis.) Later she leaves her hotel at night and gets lost in the surrounding streets. Her wanderings are indicated by her crossing the screen twice, first from right to left, then from left to right, against the same perfectly abstract black background. Near the end of the film, finally, when she has run out of money and is evicted from her last hotel room, she goes to a railway embankment and stares down at some train tracks visible through an iron fence in a series of shots and reverse shots. "I passed by some railroad tracks," the commentary says. The sound of an approaching train grows louder and louder, yet when the reverse angle shows the tracks, they are rusted and overgrown with grass. The sound of the train then grows louder still, so loud in fact that the rest of the voice-over is nearly inaudible. "But they must not have been used for a long time," her voice then adds.

Although I feel that I have succeeded in describing the film's structural complexity, I am not so certain that I have accounted for the qualities that make *Une Simple histoire* a masterpiece. Although the poetic force of such scenes as those in the café and overlooking the railroad tracks seems evident even when described in simple technical terms, there is almost no way to describe the astonishing performance of Micheline Bezançon, an actress as unjustly neglected today as the film itself; nor does there seem to be any way to give the reader any idea of the extraordinary beauty of her delivery of a text that on paper might seem flat and even simple-minded.

"Attentive viewers" who do not like the film (and generally those who find it not to their taste scoff at it or hate it with a passion) usually object to the subject, which they find puerile, sentimental, saccharine, or trivial. When it comes to judging a truly cinematic work, that is to say a work multiple in dimension and formally exhaustive in treatment, to take issue with the subject is to commit a great error. After all, are not the subjects of *Crime and Punishment* and *Macbeth* just as trivial when reduced to their bare outlines? The manner in which the subject is formally developed is what makes them masterpieces; and the same is true of *Une Simple histoire*.

The film ought to be given wider distribution. Surely in each generation of film-makers, there are two or three minds capable of grasping its enormous, indeed incalculable significance (as did Jacques Becker, who saw it while in the process of filming his own masterpiece, *Le Trou*). Hanoun's absolutely rigorous attitude vis-à-vis the material he was treating is exemplary, and material here means the sum total of faces, words, gestures, sounds, images, shot and scale changes, and so on, a whole in which every element is, a priori, absolutely equal in importance and in which *everything* plays a functional role in the plastic organization of the film. The organization he thus achieves is admittedly empirical, but in the last analysis only an empirical organization can attain in film that complete organic articulation that thus far in the history of cinema only Marcel Hanoun has achieved with his "Simple Story."[6]

Notes

1. Although practically never shown publicly, even in Paris, this film was taken up at one point by radical French literary and film critics (especially those involved with the magazines *Tel Quel* and *Cinéthique*) who considered it a fundamental break with bourgeois representational film-making. I have decided to keep this somewhat polemical passage not so much on account of its polemical character, but because I feel it tackles a fundamental miscon-

ception, one that has been cropping up in much recent "advanced" European film-making (cf. in particular *Fata Morgana* by Werner Herzog).

2. Existing in this embryonic state in almost any commercial film.

3. The special importance assumed by the cut when it occurs within a context otherwise characterized by prolonged shots is quite apparent in the work of Kenji Mizoguchi, the director who has unquestionably used the plastic potential *within* each individual shot to the greatest advantage. In most of his films, however—*The Love of Actress Sumako* (1947) is a notable exception—he seems to pay almost no attention to the transitions *between* shots. In *The Life of O'Haru*, his masterpiece, only some five or six transitions seem to make any functional use at all of the privileged position they occupy, terminating as they do very long shots. Preoccupied with the skillful reframings at which he excels, Mizoguchi simply ends a shot when there is nothing more he feels he can do with it, continuing on to the next shot just as one might turn the pages of a picture book. The important thing to be pointed out here, however, is that the more prolonged the shot is, the more apparent this quite shocking neglect becomes. This serves to underline a basic fact: the longer the shot, the more important the manner in which the film-maker cuts to the next shot.

4. Another formal approach not without analogies to twelve-tone music.

5. A technique, however, that the great pioneer film-maker Léonce Perret had thought up as early as 1912!

6. Today I have to admit that this is something of an exaggeration. For although I still feel that few directors have achieved what Hanoun did achieve, I would now add one or two other films here, in particular, Dreyer's *Vampyr*, a film that at the time of writing I scarcely knew.

6

On the Structural Use of Sound

The fundamental dialectic in film, the one that at least empirically seems to contain every other, is that contrasting and joining sound with image. The *necessary* interrelationship of sound and image today appears to be definitely established fact, as even the most doubting critic must concede once he has examined the history of film. From the very beginnings of our art, starting with Méliès's showings of his films in the basement of a Paris café, audiences and film-makers alike felt the need for some sort of sound (that is, musical) background for these images whose *silence* was unbearable,[1] despite the fact that it was this very silence that was the source of a great dramatic art now unfortunately lost.[2]

Robert Bresson, commenting on his own film practice, has made some rather revealing and pertinent remarks on the dichotomy of sound and image.[3] According to this film-maker, sound, because of its greater realism, is infinitely more evocative than an image, which is essentially only a stylization of visual reality. "A sound always evokes an image; an image never evokes a sound," Bresson contends, and he then goes on to state, with just a touch of false naïveté, that he replaces an image with a sound whenever possible, thus remaining completely faithful to the principle of maximum bareness and spareness underlying his creative method.

But is this the real essence of the problem of the relationship between sound and image? Aside from the fact that Bresson's second tenet does not really seem to follow from the first, I am not entirely certain that sound is as realistic as all that, although it certainly can be. Gregory Markopoulos's film *Twice a Man*, for instance, is preceded by some five minutes of sound effects that half the audience is apt to describe as falling rain and the other half as a crowd applauding. Obviously the image could help us decide, but as it happens the screen is blacked out, so that the sound in effect occurs off screen and is therefore precisely the sort of sound Bresson maintains can replace an image. As this example indicates, the ease with which a sound can be "deciphered" can vary as much as the ease with which the image can be "read." An extreme auditory "close-up" of a drop of water dripping into a sink is as difficult to recognize for what it really is as an extreme visual close-up of the joint of a woman's thumb (see *Geography of the Body* by Willard Maas). Any sound engineer can tell us how difficult it is to make certain sounds seem "natural," particularly if they occur off screen—that is to say, without the explanatory support furnished by the image. Bresson himself always uses easily identifiable off-screen sounds such as footsteps and creaking doors, thereby considerably limiting his sound palette. And Bresson's contention notwithstanding, a face or landscape filmed without extraneous "effects," although always a stylization of reality, as we are aware *after the fact*, will seem just as "realistic" as a door we merely hear creaking on the sound track. The evocatory effect of sound seems to me to relate more to the powers of suggestion inherent in off-screen space in everything relating to it: An off-screen glance is just as evocative. There does not seem to me to be anything *inherently* evocative in the nature of sound, even if off-screen space is obviously frequently brought to life through the sound track.

It seems that the essential nature of the relationship between sound and image is due not to the difference between them, but rather to the similarity between them. A previous chapter described how a camera's nonselectivity contrasts with the natural process of selection of the human eye, and the consequence to be deduced from this fact: the need to consider each composition as a totality. There is a similar difference between the way the human ear hears and the way a microphone records. As an example, we might use a conversation taking place inside a moving car. In a real-life situation such as this, it is usually quite easy to ignore any sounds that might interfere with our comprehension (the noise of the motor, the wind, the radio, and so on) and grasp what our fellow passengers are saying *despite* such sounds. A microphone recording the same conversation under the same conditions could not distinguish between the different sounds, however, and would jumble them all together;[4] and the sounds emerging from the single source of the loud-speaker in the theater would all be equally "present," much as a camera reduces the three-dimensionality of real space to the two-dimensionality of screen space.

Just as a game in progress on a pinball machine cannot be filmed in a comprehensible manner without somehow toning down the surface reflections on the glass above, so too the possibilities of recording a comprehensible conversation in a car are rather slight. For such a conversation to be understandable, background noises and dialogue must be recorded separately and their relative levels determined during the sound mix.[5]

Because of the "equal presence" of all the sound components of a film as they are channeled through the "funnel" of the loud-speaker in the theater, an over-all "musical "orchestration of all the distinct elements of the sound track seems to be imperative, in somewhat the same manner that the way in which a visual image is perceived demands that constant attention be paid to the total visual composition.

As has already been indicated in Chapter 4, there are certain dialectical possibilities inherent in the very nature of the sound track, not unlike the "photographic" dialectics already discussed. I shall now attempt to draw up a list of these.

The example of the car presupposes the existence of at least two different kinds of *auditory material*, "live" or "synchronous" sound on the one hand and recomposed sound produced by a mix—two types of sound that unquestionably provide the two poles of a dialectic similar to those dialectics of materials already discussed in reference to the visual image and bearing a great resemblance to one of them in particular. This sound dialectic would normally occur in conjunction with the dialectical alternation of "live" and "staged" shots and reinforce it. In actual practice, however, "improvised" shots are often completely post-synchronized ("dubbed") in a sound studio, whereas carefully staged shots are often accompanied by background sounds recorded live. Generally, it is a question of mere convenience: The director simply chooses the handiest means available to make the scenes being filmed as "lifelike" and as comprehensible as possible. Nonetheless, a complex interaction among these four poles is quite conceivable, and it might well become an essential underlying pattern for a new kind of film (I shall discuss this possibility in more detail in Chapter 7, when I take up the subject of the manipulation of chance). Even now, alternations between live and reconstituted sound occurring in conjunction with the corresponding visual alternations provide certain television programs with a very simple yet very effective structural framework. A transition from the noiseless environment of a sound stage or sound studio to the chaotic bustle of life in a shot taken in the street enormously enhances the viewer's awareness of the sudden break implicit in such a transition. This break, moreover, is experienced in an infinitely more *physical* manner than would have been the case had one carefully controlled shot been followed by one only a little less carefully controlled, if only because of the sudden tremendous increase in both the area and the indeterminacy of the off-screen space. The ambient silence a studio provides is one of the principles underlying studio recording, in fact; sounds are then introduced into it in such a way as to make our awareness of off-screen space as clear and simple as possible; and the greater or lesser differentiation of off-screen space provides another possible way of interrelating the various dialectics.

Another essential sound parameter results from the *apparent microphone distance*. A number of very complex auditory phenomena, the most important being resonance or "echo," are what determine the apparent distance between the recording microphone and the sound source (or more accurately, between this source and the theater loud-speaker, usually located just behind the screen). Structural interactions between auditory and visual space can be created rather easily through the use of this parameter, and significant but isolated attempts to do so exist in the contemporary film. (The very fact that such attempts are relatively rare provides yet another proof of my contention that sound experimentation is at least ten years be-hind other areas of investigation of the formal possibilities of film; the reasons for this will be examined at the end of this chapter.)

The long shots of a couple walking on the beach and talking to each other in a sound close-up in Agnès Varda's *La Pointe courte* provide perhaps a rather rudimentary example of the manner in which a sound "presence" can counterpoint a visual one. Orson Welles in his *Othello*, however, by emphasizing and even exaggerat-ing the congruency of auditory presence and visual presence, has creatively demonstrated the dynamic possibilities inherent in juxta-positions of extreme close-ups and long shots. Extreme close-ups are associated with an extremely intimate sound "presence," the long shots with an exaggerated booming echo, and the sharp contrast be-tween them serves as one of the elements of the deliberately jerky *découpage* of this film, already mentioned in Chapter 3.

Another form of interaction between visual space and sound presence perhaps even richer in potential can be found in Mizogu-chi's *The Crucified Lovers*, a film that even today remains at the very forefront of experimentation in the relations of sound and image. Toward the end of the film, prior to the lovers' final cap-ture, when Sessame's brother steals off to get the police, the silence that attends his slipping away into the distance is suddenly inter-rupted by a musical motif played fortissimo, percussively, on the zither-like *samisen* in extreme sound close-up. The contrast between the remoteness of the visual "subject" and the close proximity of the sound "subject" produces an extremely startling effect; it is almost as if a new character had suddenly appeared in the shot in an ex-treme visual close-up, although it is precisely the absence of any new visual presence in the area close to the camera and the resulting *sur-prise*[6] that makes this moment such a dramatically tense one.

It will be noticed that, concerning the modes of interaction be-tween the various sound materials as well as those between auditory and visual space, I make no distinction between music, dialogue, and sound effects. These two types of dialectical interaction can in fact involve any sort of sound. Shared as it is by a small but growing minority of film-makers these days, this attitude brings the ultimate aim of contemporary experiments in the use of sound a step closer to realization: the creation, that is, of a coherent, organically structured sound track in which the forms of interaction between sound and image will be closely tied to other interactions between the three basic types of film sounds: dialogue; music; and sound effects, whether identifiable or not. Mizoguchi's[7] *The Crucified Lovers* is a pioneer effort in this direction as well. The particular quality of Japanese music (to be discussed further below) with its predominance of abrupt percussive sounds and its eminently "graphic" structures obviously made it easier to create some form of interaction between sound effects and music. Yet, even granting the advantage Japanese music confers, Mizoguchi's sound track is a unique achievement in the history of cinema. In a scene in which the hero hides in an attic, a succession of sounds with a distinct rhythm of their own created by the wooden bowls from which the hero has been eating, then by a ladder banging against the wall, provide the first notes (of somewhat indeterminate pitch) in a musically orchestrated structure that goes on to incorporate instruments with tone qualities similar to those of these "natural" sound effects. Another musical passage ends on a "note" that in fact is the sound of a door closing in frame. Aside from the organic, dialectical link established in this way between "functional" sound effects and music, the very fact that the sound effects are synchronous with a visual image results in other interactions, this time between the images and the entire sound tissue of the film, which at times shifts without a break from an off-screen to an on-screen "presence."

Another possible relationship between sound, particularly music, and image (a dialectical relationship in so far as it periodically draws sound and image together) involves the creation of an *analogy* between them. A scene of struggle in a bamboo thicket is accompanied by a brief flurry of sounds made on instruments similar to woodblocks that are strongly suggestive of the sounds that might result were one to tap on the bamboo stalks filling the screen. It is difficult to conceive of this approach ever leading to any very substantial developments, yet Eisenstein considered this a very important form of interaction (as exemplified in the coronation scene in *Ivan the Terrible*, where the close-up of the imperial globe is accompanied by an extremely low and resonant bass note), just as he attributed great importance to all other forms of analogy between sound and image, as his analysis of Prokofiev's score of *Alexander Nevsky* indicates.

Let us now return to a possibility suggested above, that of integrating sound effects and music into a single sound texture. Obviously dialogue, the third form of sound, can also play a role in creating such a relationship. Once again, there is no doubt that Japanese theatrical diction, with its shrieking, panting, rumbling sounds constituting a tonal range similar to that of Schoenbergian *Sprachgesang*, is particularly capable of organically interacting with other forms of sound so as to create a single complex sound texture. Mizoguchi (in *The Crucified Lovers* and other films) and Kurosawa (notably in *The Lower Depths* and *The Hidden Fortress*) have explored some of the possibilities of "musically" orchestrating dialogue, if not specifically incorporating them into the over-all sound complex. Yet it is Joseph von Sternberg, approaching the Japanese language "from the outside" (the dialogue in *The Saga of Anatahan* is not supposed to be comprehensible to the audience), who most consciously exploited the resources of that language, sometimes closely coupled with stylized sound effects, to create purely auditory patterns.

Nonetheless the most interesting attempt to treat dialogue as both the vehicle for the dramatic action and musically organized sound is Abraham Polonsky's "film maudit," *Force of Evil*. Here the entire dialogue takes the form of alliterations, dissonant rhymes, and rhythmical effects of every sort, even at times serving as a sort of "relay" for the sound effects, as when knocks on a door repeat the rhythm and timbre of the preceding line of dialogue.

In the examples thus far cited, sound effects, even when treated in close dialectical association with music or dialogue, have in each case been related in some manner either to an event seen on screen or or to an off-screen event linked in some way to the action and playing some role in it (as the sea-shell curtains in *Anatahan* or the knocks on the door in *Force of Evil* do). Certain sound technicians, however, have explored the possibility of treating sound effects much more freely, giving them the role the musical score purportedly plays in most films that have one. The person in France to have most systematically experimented with this approach is Michel Fano, a composer turned sound engineer and then film-maker, but whose attention is primarily directed toward what his Brazilian counterparts refer to as "audioplastics"—that is, with the conception and technical execution of the entire sound complex, during not only the editing but also the actual shooting as well, in so far as preconceived sound structures can determine certain visual components. Michel Fano's most interesting work has been in collaboration with Alain Robbe-Grillet, whose films represent the most exhaustive and thoroughgoing attempts I know of to organize musically off-screen sound. Mizoguchi, as we have seen, created a sound texture in which visually identifiable on-screen sounds synchronous with the image were intimately associated with musical elements (occurring by definition, off screen), these two sound parameters being linked through similarities in tone quality as well. Although among the first to realize the importance of the use of sound in *The Crucified Lovers*, Michel Fano nonetheless proceeds in an altogether different manner. He often starts with a visual element (the garage or the harbor in *L'Immortelle*, for instance) and then progressively incorporates off-screen sounds into the sound track, organizing them into "musical" structures—hammer blows supposedly coming from the garage, a concert of sirens from the ships in the harbor—thereby contrasting a highly articulated and "graphic" off-screen auditory space with the plastic and dynamic organization of the images.

This extreme stylization of off-screen sound (in which synchronous elements can function as rhythmical punctuation—the pneumatic train doors and the hardware store chimes in *Trans-Europ-Express* are two notable examples) is achieved through the organization of real-life sounds (usually left just as they are or tinkered with only a little bit) into structures that, if not exactly serial (the sounds involved often being of indeterminate pitch and in any case untempered), nevertheless are quite similar to the strategies of contemporary music.

Fano thus far has not included all three types of sound (sound effects, music, and dialogue) as components, nor has he established the constant "relays" with the image that are needed if the full *dialectical* implications of this type of organization of sound are ever to be realized. This would obviously require the total collaboration of film-maker and sound engineer throughout every stage of the conception and execution of a film.[8] A first step has nonetheless been taken, and there is no reason why a film-maker should not some day be able to create a vast dialectical interaction between sound and image by applying, among others, the principles of serial organization to his *découpage*, exploiting, on the one hand, the various temporal and spatial dialectics we have outlined, and, on the other, the possible forms of combining the three types of sound and integrating the resulting auditory configurations with the film's over-all plastic conception.

Fano is not altogether alone in his research in this direction. When Jacques Rivette asked Jean-Claude Éloy to create the sound effects and music for *The Nun*, he indicated his interest in this kind of experimentation. And a group of young Brazilians, working notably with Pereira dos Santos on his *Vidas secas*, have shown talent and sensitivity to the plastic organization of sounds motivated by the image (as particularly demonstrated by the incredible beauty of the prolonged creaking of a cartwheel that serves as a "musical" accompaniment to the credit sequence in this film).

The accomplishments of these young Brazilians, however, also reflect the desire on the part of a large number of film-makers to eliminate entirely any sort of traditional music score, believing as they do that more or less structured sound effects,[9] possibly combined with musical themes drawn from our classical musical heritage (as, for example, the use of fragments from *La Traviata* in *Trans-Europ-Express* or motifs from Beethoven's quartets in *Une Femme mariée*) can and should replace what in their eyes is a totally discredited convention. In view of the very bad uses to which musical scores have been put in the sound film, this attitude can easily be defended. Nevertheless, to reject categorically the possibility of complete auditory stylization that music provides is to deprive oneself somewhat arbitrarily of a raw material that, when properly approached, can lead to an undeniable enrichment of a film. Without its musical score, *The Crucified Lovers*, for instance, would be a rather minor work. For, no matter how moving Chikamatsu's story is, the film is far from the plastic equal of *Sansho the Bailiff* or *The Life of O'Haru*; it is the score and the sound effects that make the film into a near masterpiece.

Films about which the same can be said are few in number, as there are few works of cinema in which music is an organic and integral part of the over-all formal texture. As I have already indicated, Japanese classical music seems particularly amenable to this sort of integration.[10] It would appear that this is due to the extremely flexible, supple, "open" quality of this music (which is not subject to the "tyranny of the bar-line" as Western music is and above all is not restricted to tonal structures) that makes it infinitely more adaptable to the eminently nonmeasurable rhythms of film "action" and film editing. Japanese music, however hieratic, seems to have a freer flow, an empirical quality closer to that of the film image. Moreover, as was mentioned in the discussion of *The Crucified Lovers*, a large number of the timbres found in Japanese music are similar to everyday sounds, thus making the organic interaction of sound effects and music suggested here easier to achieve.

What might a Western film-maker conclude from these observations? The generalized use of Japanese music in its pure state is obviously not possible in Western cinema. One revealing fact, however, might be pointed out here: Japanese music was not really accessible to the Western ear until after the introduction of atonal music; young serial composers see profound affinities between their work and classical Japanese music, as would not have been the case with any Western musician before Debussy.

Serial music, then, the most "open" form in the history of Western music, with its unprecedented rhythmical freedom and its use of timbres that classical musicians considered vulgar noises, seems uniquely suited to organic, dialectical integration of music with sound effects, as well as with the filmed image, whereas traditional tonal music with its predetermined forms, its strong tonal polarities, and its range of relatively homogeneous tone colors can provide only an autonomous continuity existing *alongside* that of the images, merely running parallel to the dialogue and sound effects or accompanying the images with a musical synchronicity of the sort found in animated cartoons.[11] Serial music, on the other hand, provides the most open form conceivable. In its interstices, every form of sound has a natural place, and it can provide an ideal complement to the "irrational" quality of the concrete image as such as well as to the more rational structures created by the *découpage*. Serial composers starting with Webern were, moreover, the first to consider silence as an essential musical component. After a long period during which the talking picture with a musical score seems to have been haunted by the terror, or perhaps the memory, of silence, young film-makers have at last begun to be aware of the dialectical role silence can play relative to sound. These film-makers have even succeeded in making a subtle yet basic distinction between the different "colors" of silence (a complete dead space on the sound track, studio silence, silence in the country, and so forth), thus glimpsing some of the structural roles such silences can play (as is particularly evident in *Deux ou trois choses que je sais d'elle*).

The reader will rightly feel that this chapter is more sketchy than some of the others. This is largely because it was written ten years too early, for, as has already been said, the evolution of film sound lags far behind that of the film image. Even in the most "advanced" contemporary films (*Une Simple histoire, Last Year at Marienbad, Nicht Versöhnt, Persona*, and others), sound plays the role of a "poor relation" of the image: From the standpoint of its inherent possibilities, it participates in the experimental search for new forms only in the most minimal sort of way. The few experimenters who could remedy this situation have thus far not been given the means with which to do so. To organize successfully and totally a sound track both internally and relative to the image, to create a total sound texture and bring every one of its components under control (by manufacturing street sounds from discrete real sounds, for instance), the amount of money budgeted for sound in an ordinary film project would have to be doubled. That subtleties of this sort should seem rather pointless to those who finance films is more or less to be expected, and thus the immediate future looks bleak. But one can always hope that the qualified experimenters will some day find the means with which to carry out successfully the formal research that is crucial if cinema is ever to realize fully its inherent potential in this area.

Notes

1. It is usually maintained that this silence was unbearable only because it allowed the noise of the projector to be heard. This silence, however, is no less painful in situations where the projector noise cannot be heard, as is the case at the Cinémathèque Française. Fritz Lang's *Mabuse* made a much greater impression on all of us when we were finally able to see it with a musical accompaniment like that provided in the days of silent film. Admittedly the music in this case is little more than sound background; nevertheless, it provides a time scale against which the "rhythms" of the *découpage* become far more concrete.

2. Garrel's completely silent film Le Révélateur, as well as many "new American" films, seem to indicate that this is not entirely true.

3. In a program in the Cinéastes de notre temps series, directed by François Weyergans.

4. Under certain conditions directional—that is, selective—microphones can remedy this, but this fact does not invalidate the present argument, at least in so far as human perception is concerned; especially when the peculiar and rather bad quality of the sound thus obtained results in merely another stylization, a phenomenon comparable to what happens to a voice heard over the telephone.

5. Godard, who is quite interested in sound interference of this sort, often records similar scenes in synchronous sound (or recreates the same effect in a studio), doubtless to make us aware of the effort our ear must make to understand whatever message is being transmitted.

6. See Chapter 8.

7. A certain amount of similar experimentation can be found, although in far less systematic form, in some of Mizoguchi's other films, notably in Story of the Late Chrysanthemums, The Life of O'Haru, and Sansho the Bailiff.

8. Just before the French edition went to press, I saw L'Homme qui ment (The Man Who Lies), the admirable outcome of all the experiments Fano had undertaken previously, a film in which the three types of sound are integrated in an almost flawless manner, although their integration with the image and the film's découpage is perhaps a bit too episodic. And of course we must now add Fano's own film on animals, Le Territoire des autres, his most important experiment to date.

9. The opposite procedure, in which musical and paramusical elements replace certain sound effects, resulting in a form of dialectics of materials, often explored when sound was first introduced (notably in Boris Barnett's Okraina, the first feature film to have a sound track based on artificial sounds, obtained by filming geometrical patterns directly on the optical track) and by Sternberg in his Saga of Anatahan, has apparently been temporarily abandoned, except for its use in purely experimental films. This dialectic nevertheless is rich in possibilities, and it will surely soon be explored again.

10. Aside from the Mizoguchi films already mentioned, other films in which this integration is partially achieved are Kon Ichikawa's Enjo and Ishida's Fallen Flowers, (1939).

11. The exceptions to this seeming general rule are few and far between. One of the most noteworthy is Giovanni Fuco's score for Cronaca di un amore, where the use of two instruments with strongly contrasting tone qualities (a saxophone and a piano, usually used separately), of a musical style closely associated with the film's découpage and even with the dialogue, and of a quite subtle musical development in which the themes consist of little more than recurring musical intervals creates a "graphic" relationship between music and film; the score in fact is one of the principal elements contributing to the film's unity.

III

Perturbing Factors

7

Chance and Its Functions

The concept of sheer chance is a very fashionable one in contemporary art, and, like every fashion, there is a very serious concern underlying it. This particular fashion sheds considerable light on one striking trend in current aesthetic theory: the many ways in which, in the West, the traditional integrity of the work of art is being challenged, and the manner in which the artist's heretofore inviolate, demiurgic role is being questioned. These explorations also extend beyond these avant-garde concerns, however, for they reflect a very widespread, although confused, impatience with the solidly established tradition of the "closed" as against the "open" work of art.

What might the terms "chance" and "open work" mean in film? In literature, theater, painting, dance, and above all music, these terms have meant, among other things, the sudden intrusion of more or less "natural" contingencies into the totally artificial world of the work of art, in which *in principle* they are completely out of place. This phenomenon occurs in cinema as well, although in an altogether different form, as we shall see further on.

At this point I shall undertake a brief survey of the use of chance in another art, music, not because I am persuaded that such techniques should be directly employed in film, but rather simply to examine what the general nature of chance in art might be, and what possible pattern of interferences there may be between the contingent and the determined. I have chosen to refer to chance in music rather than in painting, literature, or dance because music lends itself most readily to an examination of the problem in abstract terms, thus clearing the way for a more concrete application of these ideas to film later in this chapter. Moreover, it is composers who have been the most deeply concerned with this problem and explored it the most systematically.

It is often said that young composers of the contemporary school are endeavoring to introduce random elements into their music, but in actual fact this is merely one of many possible aleatory techniques, and what is more, it appears to be the most dubious, or, if the reader prefers, the most radical of any currently being employed in their art. Those giving themselves over to experiments of this sort are divided into two groups, which occasionally overlap. There are those, first, who introduce into the work as it is being performed a contingent world completely beyond both the composer's and the performer's control, its relationship to the work consequently being totally fortuitous. John Cage and his "prepared piano" provide an example: He places on the piano strings various loose objects, which move about during the performance, thus distorting the tonalities of the instrument in an absolutely unpredictable manner; some of his young German disciples provoke audience reactions, which are then "incorporated" into the work being performed, somewhat in the manner of a happening. As I have said, this constitutes the most radical approach to the aleatoric, the joyful and lucid abandonment by the composer of a portion of his conscious control over the work.

This temptation, however, to "let go of the reins," to relinquish control, is also felt by other composers, with one crucial difference: They prefer to see the breath of sheer chance—that is to say, of the purely accidental—pass over their work *before* it is placed before the public. Cage has composed music by flipping a coin ("Music of Changes"), and a few contemporary composers, the best known in France being Ianis Xenakis, have gone so far as to entrust certain decisions regarding composition to computers. We are obviously confronted here with the notorious notion of "controlled chance"—one that can conceal a good deal of confused thinking. When a listener asked Xenakis whether he deliberately tampered with the results he obtained from his computers, the composer is reported to have replied, "Yes, for aesthetic reasons."(!)

However, any film-maker, in particular, can attest to the fascination experienced by a creative artist when he contemplates and "displays" objects or materials that he himself has not created and that strike him as being all the more beautiful simply because they are not a product of his talent (that is, Man, the Artist, is not their Creator). One thinks here of Marcel Duchamp's "ready-mades." He can also attest to the even greater satisfaction the artist experiences when he *reworks* materials and objects of this kind, deliberately integrating them with others of his own creation, reincorporating them into a closed work—in short, snatching them from the slag heap of the accidental where they originated and preserving throughout the unique originality of these materials fallen from another world, as in Schwitters's collages.

However, the forms in which chance predominantly occurs in contemporary music, mainly because they are the forms the aleatoric takes in the works of the most respected composers, has nothing at all to do with the random. These types of chance enter into the elaboration of "open" works—ones, that is, capable of assuming a multiplicity of forms, either through the sharing of creative responsibilities (as in improvisation within predetermined limits) or through the incorporation of "alternatives" in the work (works with a variable rather than a fixed mode of performance, with interchangeable movements, and so on), or, more frequently, through a combination of both approaches.

On several occasions, I have established parallels between the potential structures of film and those currently being effectively employed in serial music. In almost every instance, anticipating possible objections, I was careful to state that analogies of this sort were valid only to a limited degree and emphasized that they should not be taken literally. It is in dealing with the problem of the aleatoric, I feel, that I will be best able to distinguish between the absolutely abstract world of music and the simultaneously abstract and concrete world of film, a distinction that should be kept in mind whenever any parallel between the two arts is suggested. Of the two different forms in which the aleatoric can occur, the first (its direct intervention in a work, whether controlled or uncontrolled) seems the more "organically relevant" to film, whereas the second (its use in the creation of works with multiple modes of performance) seems to be the more relevant to music. The formal strategy involved in creating a work with multiple itineraries, regardless of whether or not the soloists are given any initiative, is a logical extension of the serial approach in general and, through it, of the entire history of Western music. No basic historical continuity is destroyed by it, while the deliberate introduction into music of completely random elements, coming from outside the sound-proof concert halls and other places where music traditionally has sought refuge, unquestionably constitutes an act of *subversion* against the very foundations of music as an art, or at least what would still appear even today to be its very foundations. The random, at least in our sense of the term, is a foreign body forcibly introduced into music.[1]

In film, however, precisely the contrary is true. Here the very idea of an open work is the "foreign body," if only because of the small number of film-makers actually advocating it. That this number should be so small might seem to be due to the technical problems involved, an explanation that is not altogether false, though these problems are not insurmountable ones and do not affect the basic point at issue at all. Several films have been projected simultaneously on the same screen or on two adjacent ones, but attempts such as these are merely frivolous, a kind of deliberate reductio ad absurdum. A more serious experiment might take the form of creating a film with multiple interchangeable facets, using differently edited versions of the same material, for instance, or perhaps by filming works with multiple itineraries on videotape, incorporating some sort of technical improvisation while they are being made. If such experiments have in fact been undertaken, they have thus far had no major repercussions. A film's integrity appears for the moment to be as fundamental to a definition of cinema as music's need to be sheltered from the random sounds of life has always been. After some ten centuries of closed works, this conception may have exhausted its seminal potentialities as far as music is concerned. The very notion of the film as a work of art, by contrast, goes back only a few decades, and it would thus be quite surprising if the time had already come to challenge this concept, simply to keep up with older and more hallowed arts, to provide oneself as it were with an as yet undeserved patent of nobility. And this is all the more true when prospects for a new type of film similar to that outlined here are just now beginning to come into view. Admittedly the sort of work we suggest will still be a closed form, but it will be one of a complexity and richness unprecedented in the entire history of art.

On the other hand, while chance per se constitutes an intrusion into the world of music,[2] the aleatory is quite at home in film and always has been. Since the very earliest days of cinema film-makers have had to put up with chance, willy-nilly. At the beginning, films were almost totally at its mercy. Lumière set his camera up on the station platform at La Ciotat and waited for the train to pull in. When it came in sight it was he who decided when to crank away behind the camera, but chance remained in complete control of the *mise-en-scène*. The bulk of the film's action consisted of *unpredictable* gestures and movements of passengers getting off the train and people waiting for them on the platform. Nevertheless, even as early as this film, one of the first ever made, Lumière had already begun that *struggle against the accidental* that was to characterize nearly all film-making for the next sixty years. The very fact that he chose to set up his camera in one spot rather than another enabled Lumière to predetermine successfully the plastic behavior of *one* of the elements in his composition, the train itself, an entirely predictable element. Both literally and figuratively, he thus established a *frame*, thereby delimiting the area in which the unpredictable remainder of the action would occur. Seeing beyond the purely negative attitude toward the accidental, and the ruthless struggle to eliminate it, Lumière had taken a first step toward its *control*. This is an idea we will come back to later. At the same time, Lumière filmed events that were completely under his control, as in *L'Arroseur arrosé* and other such films—a huge step "forward" in which the accidental is kept outside the frame as much as possible, relegated to some vague and remote off-screen space from which it will only occasionally and timidly re-emerge, until its rehabilitation some sixty years later. Lumière's films such as these were, in short, the beginning of *mise-en-scène*.

The battle against the accidental was not won immediately— chance had to be overcome in all its manifestations, and in certain cases only technical progress could successfully bring the contingent under control. In any case, the film studio gradually became the refuge of an art seeking to escape the accidental, for it furnished an environment in which everything could be more and more perfectly controlled, thanks to increasingly refined techniques. Efforts in this direction eventually led directors to adopt the British independent frame, confining both actors and technicians within the strait jacket of the *storyboard*, and (in the United States especially) to replace actual location shooting with more and more elaborate special effects (mats, background plates, Dunnings, traveling mats, and other techniques allowing actors and background to be filmed separately), making it almost entirely unnecessary ever to venture outside a studio where random intrusions can often only be prevented through the expenditure of enormous sums of money. It is worth noting that this overcoming, or rather *banishing*, of the accidental developed hand in hand with the progressive enthronement of that "zero point of cinematic style," which, as stated earlier, was aimed principally at rendering technique invisible but also at eliminating any "defects" resulting from chance intrusions of any sort. As we shall soon see, it is not altogether an accident that the rediscovery of the contingent and the renewed rejection of that "zero point of cinematic style" should have occurred at almost the same moment in the history of cinema.

I have perhaps created the false impression that I believe that every film-maker from Lumière on is a rabid enemy of chance, that all film-makers yield to the intrusions of the accidental only against their will. Although it is true that the most creative function of chance has only been understood very recently through the work of film-makers such as Godard and Rouch, some directors of exceptional insight had nonetheless already anticipated the function chance might fulfill in the realm of film syntax. At least as early as 1920, a number of directors made no attempt to prevent the intrusion of chance. On the contrary, they were quite willing largely to subordinate their camera to the aleatory world they referred to as "reality." This group was of course the first generation of great documentary film-makers: Dziga Vertov, Joris Ivens, Walther Ruttman, Alberto Cavalcanti, and others. It would never have occurred to them however to refer to *L'Entrée d'un train en gare de la Ciotat* as an aleatory film, nor would it to the contemporary "leftist" historian of cinema: To both, it is simply the first film to "bear witness." In part, this is a matter of vocabulary, but it is chiefly a value judgment. When there is a revolution to carry out in the Soviet Union or bring about in other countries, one can hardly allow oneself to dwell at length on the aesthetic implications of permanently capturing the unpredictable on film, of transforming chance into an aesthetic object. If one shares this ethical bias, films have a precise function, a social function: They should be windows open on the world, and so on. However, when we see the astounding stylistic experimentation being carried out in a propaganda film such as Dziga Vertov's *Enthusiasm*, we have a sneaking suspicion that despite possible misgivings he has been unable to resist the aesthete's fascination for creative new techniques of his own devising.[3]

This attraction is quite normal, for Vertov was above all else an editor, as, to a lesser extent, were all the great creators of the Soviet silent film. In the peace and quiet of the cutting room, the editor has always been the first to reflect on the extraordinary variety of material that the world of chance, once captured on film, provides him and the creative power of his scissors. Even in the case of the most meticulously "staged" films, the editor will soon notice that minor accidents completely beyond the control of the director, who was not able even to see them during the shooting, have given him an opportunity to create a very strong articulation between two shots.

Having become aware of this, certain film-makers began to approach the shooting, particularly of action scenes, from an entirely different perspective. Through the proper choice of lenses and camera setups, the film-maker would simply demarcate a framed area inside which events were permitted to unfold in only a partly controllable manner, so that the film result would consist of something known beforehand to include thousands of "valences," such a large number of possible "interesting" matches that restructuring the action through the editing would become the film-maker's essential task, the stage in the creative process in which he could truly exercise his will, with a freedom that depended largely on the range of possibilities he had left open during the shooting stage. As early as *Strike*, Eisenstein shot the sequence with the firehoses from very carefully chosen camera angles, which, although they did not give him control over the actual details of composition (seemingly impossible in a scene involving so many imponderable factors), nonetheless would later afford him innumerable possible matches between the images thus deliberately "provoked" (through reversals in the angles of the water spouts, crowd movements in opposite directions, and so on). Conceivably, this same activity could have been meticulously staged shot by shot, but in such a case not only would the participants' acting have appeared less dramatic, but the editing in particular would have been infinitely less flexible and rewarding to the eye. In such a situation, the accidental in fact provides far more subtle and more complex cutting possibilities than any film-maker can foresee (or could at that time at any rate). In the scene in *October* where the buxom bourgeois women in their rustling laces poke out the young sailor's eyes with the tips of their umbrellas, Eisenstein brings the camera right up to the action and follows it very closely, aware that, in addition to the intrinsic beauty of the shots thus obtained, this kaleidoscopic flurry of dancing silhouettes, whirling cloth, and dripping blood will result in a cascade of images, visible in all their detail only in the developed film, for the cameraman himself will not even have seen them as he views the action through his small eyepiece (a feather boa visible on screen for a few fractions of a second, a flare frame only a few inches long), aware that these "accidents" will later afford him the possibility of cutting to another shot in a visually interesting way at almost any frame. Having all but entirely relinquished control during the shooting and thus left certain of his prerogatives in the hands of chance, the film-maker regained the control he had surrendered a hundred-fold in the editing; he had ensnared chance, so to speak. The accidental had been given free rein and yielded everything it could as the actors performed more or less spontaneously and the camera froze it all into a succession of minute frames, sixteen to the second. The film-maker could then proceed to *choose* among many possible matches, and it was precisely this great number of possibilities that, in the final analysis, allowed him to dominate chance rather than be dominated by it (as would have been the case if, for example, this scene had been filmed in a single unedited shot).

All this might seem to be belaboring the obvious: Film, it may be objected, has always involved a series of compromises between the accidental and the deliberately controlled. True enough. Yet it is also, and mainly, a matter of degree—and of a director's basic approach. There are those, as we have pointed out, who have always done their utmost to eliminate random elements, and a great number of others who have paid some tribute to chance, although not all of these have done so in the same spirit. There are those who only apparently allowed it to play a part, their principle concern being to banish the genuinely contingent and replace it with a *semblance* of sheer chance. This practice is particularly characteristic of the group of British directors whose films for the General Post Office Film Unit gives us apparently spontaneous scenes; these scenes are not exactly recreations, professionally acted on sets (the settings and people were "real"), but the mail sorters on the Glasgow train (*Night-Mail*) who were playing their everyday roles for the camera did so in carefully lit, carefully planned situations. A second group, including a majority of Hollywood directors, compromise with chance in a completely pragmatic and even opportunistic way. They learned from the Russian film-makers that violent action or "mob scenes" turned out best if shot according to the "probabilistic method," and followed their example.

The Americans' hardheaded practicality also led them, however, to employ a similar approach in situations where it does not "pay off" nearly as well. They developed the stereotyped shot and reverse shot method of shooting (with each scene filmed several times from several different angles and distances), which seemed to give them more freedom in the cutting stage, for it allowed them to choose the shot best setting off the *acting*. This approach, nonetheless, resulted in a limited range of *plastic* possibilities during editing, for it eliminated almost all the formal relationships of possible interest in such scenes, which would have been better served had the shots been set up and filmed in a more complex fashion, since it is always possible to cope with acting problems through multiple takes. The "zero point of cinematic style" conditioned their limited view of chance. A whole cinematic tradition, in fact, pretends to favor intrusions of the accidental, but this tradition does not view chance as a totality of events of every possible kind, whether dramatically expressive or simply plastic, capable of being captured and fixed on film, but rather as having almost entirely to do with the performance of the actors. The American shot and reverse shot technique was, and essentially remains, a method conceived as a way of enveloping the actors from every side, establishing a formal composition of a minimum complexity within which they may be fairly spontaneous, and even go so far as to completely improvise (it was probably the Marx brothers who have derived the most advantage from the freedom this shooting method offers).

For almost thirty years, then, the problem of the degree of control over the image captured on film was posed exclusively in terms of its expressive "content," in terms of the actor and the dialogue—director X perhaps allowing his actors to improvise somewhat, director Y perhaps preferring to shoot scenes with actors in the street with concealed cameras to make them appear more lifelike.[4] The Eisensteinian notion that the aleatory could actually affect form as well as content does not appear to have interested anyone in feature film-making based on fictional subjects except Eisenstein himself. Even in his sound films, seemingly less experimental in form than his silent films, whenever he confronted material the least bit beyond his control, Eisenstein devoted himself to creating a second very extensive cinematic material out of this "real" raw material. He used every possible angle and camera-subject distance when filming the chance fragment, with only a general idea in his mind of how these angles and shot sizes would interact together, the actual articulations between shots being determined to a large extent by the thousand and one "accidents" detectable only on the editing table.[5]

Outside of fiction film-making, this approach was adopted by numerous Scandinavian and English-speaking documentary film-makers who soon realized that the more or less uncontrollable reality that interested them could best be approached in this manner. But their attitude came closer to a newsreel editor's in so far as during the actual shooting they were nowhere close to having as clear a conception of how the footage would eventually be edited as the Russian master had. They therefore found themselves confronted in the editing room with material that had been insufficiently "preconditioned" (as also occurred in the case of almost every director who attempted to adopt Eisenstein's method when filming their "action" scenes). Perhaps this is why the films that resulted so often have a gratuitous air about them, rather complex structures at times having been grafted onto formal and/or ideational statements that were singularly undistinguished. In Eisenstein's work on the other hand, the poetry of structures is an essential part of the film's statement, particularly in those sequences in which controlled chance occurs in some form or other, sequences in which visual texture and statement seem to emerge simultaneously (in the famous Odessa steps sequence, in particular). Eisenstein of course worked only with material that he could at least partially control. Some form of partial control is even an essential feature of his method, and the creator of *Ivan the Terrible* can scarcely be imagined going out into the streets camera in hand. The parallel here established between Eisenstein and the documentary film-makers of the 1930's might thus appear to be somewhat unjustified and even unfair to these latter (who in fact made some quite respectable films), but the fact remains that documentary film-makers are almost the only Western directors to have been influenced (for good or ill) by Eisenstein and the other great Russians[6] as well as being almost the only ones who have claimed to be disciples of his. Directors of the fiction film had to undergo a good many other shocks—including television—before they were to become at all aware that a great many positive advantages could result from something every film-maker discovers early in his career: that *film material is always refractory to some degree.*

Over the last fifty years or so, film directors essentially attempted to eliminate, as much as possible, any intrusion of mere chance, of the contingencies of everyday reality. Only relatively recently has anyone become interested in aiming a camera at this uncontrollable world, not only for sociopolitical and informational purposes but also with the awareness that, out of this confrontation between camera and contingent reality, new forms and new structures could result, either by further developing, through editing, material filmed in such a way as to respect its profoundly *accidental* nature (something the old school of documentary film-makers never succeeded in doing) or, even more importantly, by incorporating chance material into other completely preplanned material. This is clearly the same sort of a dialectical interaction between different types of material (such as practiced by Godard) that is described in Chapter 4, although it is seen here from a slightly different perspective.

One of the most important insights to have come from television was the realization that the camera's relationship to this imperfectly controllable, "spontaneous" chance reality was not necessarily that of a spectator: The camera could also participate in a reciprocal exchange. This discovery was the source of *cinéma vérité* in all its manifestations and, in general, of a whole new world of narrative forms involving shifts in the role of the camera (from actual participant to passive spectator, from a mere "provocateur" of events to active dictator of them, and so on) as a formal and structural device, as the very basis of film discourse.

Shirley Clarke's film based on the play *The Connection* provides a *simulation* of this dialectical use of shifting camera roles (for in this film the camera is never a genuine participant in the action; and it is even doubtful whether any real improvisation occurred before it). Nevertheless, the form of the film derives from the possibilities revealed by true *cinéma vérité*, and from this point of view it remains very instructive. For example, during a prolonged long shot, quite ostentatiously *composed* (the camera as a "dictator" of the action), an actor suddenly turns toward the lens and takes the cameraman to task, bringing about an actual shift in the camera's role, for it suddenly becomes a *participant* in the middle of the shot. Later, the camera even becomes a kind of *passive voyeur*, when the cameraman has had a "fix" and the lens wanders idly over the walls. The implications of these shifts extend far beyond the importance of the play and even of the film itself; they have apparently borne fruit even in Europe, particularly in *L'Amour fou* by Jacques Rivette, who is a known admirer of Shirley Clarke's work. He has gone further however and employed true shifts in the camera's role.

Jean Rouch's use of shifts in the relationship between camera and characters in *Moi, un noir* is tremendously complex; any examination of them on the basis of the finished film is quite problematic. The very solid structural framework of the film highlights the apparently completely chance nature of the original material by comparison with the "finished" quality of the spectacle we see. In actual fact, however, the original material, far from being homogeneous, has several levels of "authenticity," combined with an artfulness unprecedented at the time (1959). The visuals, shot silent, consist of scenes alternately more or less staged, more or less improvised, or more or less actually lived; in the first two instances, there is some degree of awareness on the actors' part of the camera's presence, whereas, in the third case, the actors are either unaware of the camera's presence or have simply forgotten it (as in the drunk scene). There are continual transitions from one form of camera-actor relationship to another, often within a single shot, resulting in an enormous variety of shifts in awareness created through visual means. But that is not all. The relationship between the protagonists and their filmed image subsequently becomes the object of similar shifts during the recording of the participants' comments on themselves. Sometimes they forget that a microphone is present, so that it becomes what might be described as an eavesdropper; sometimes they remember, and the microphone then becomes a participant. The whole formal development of *Moi, un noir* hinges on these constantly shifting relationships between actors and the instruments recording their actions, and the result constitutes one of the most remarkable examples of the use of sheer happenstance as a formal dimension.

In the wake of these pioneering efforts in France, several filmmakers of the New York underground have attempted to exploit shifts in the camera's role. Aside from the somewhat unusual film by Shirley Clarke that I have already mentioned, the most interesting of these attempts is Andy Warhol's *The Chelsea Girls*. This film, at the time of its making, was undoubtedly one of the most radical versions of the filmed "psychodrama" (Jean Rouch and Edgar Morin being more "academic" proponents of this sort of work in their *Cronique d'un été*). Its great originality lies in shifts in the camera's role (sometimes a voyeur, sometimes a participant, sometimes a "distancing" device through the use of jerky pans and zooms, sometimes merely a director's tool determining what is seen on screen through very conventional setups), these many shifts effectively suggesting the ambivalence of the roles assumed by the characters themselves (is the beautiful girl really a male transvestite, or is she a lesbian playing at being one, or is she perhaps a "straight" who has been asked to play a lesbian playing a transvestite, and so on?).[7] The film is a perpetual interplay of masks, in which the viewer finds it absolutely impossible to determine the part played by improvisation (whether free or within predetermined limits), the part played by the acting out of previously agreed-on gestures, and even the number of lines of dialogue actually decided on beforehand. Despite, or rather because of, this constant ambiguity on every level, *The Chelsea Girls* possesses an unusual tension, often maintained throughout an entire sequence and often considerably heightened by the fact that each of the film's twelve sequences lasts as long as the film-magazine in the camera (thirty minutes). The extraordinarily prolonged continuity that results also makes certain kinds of shifts in camera role possible (as, for example, from a voyeur to an actual instrument of torture when a harassed participant in the psychodrama walks over to the footage counter to determine how long this harassment will continue).

As for the "open" form taken by the film as a whole (two reels simultaneously projected on two adjacent screens with more or less random alternation between their sound tracks), it is so elementary a procedure compared with the richness and complexity of the material generated by the interplay of masks that only a few striking but isolated plastic effects produced by the fortuitous juxtaposition of two images seem worth remembering. In this respect, the film seems to confirm to some extent what was stated at the beginning of this chapter: Although some form of interaction involving sheer chance may prove very worth while in film, the concept of an "open" work is for the moment totally irrelevant to the essential problems of the medium.

The accidental also intervenes in *The Chelsea Girls* in another way that is just as intriguing. The feeling that there is a truly uncontrollable world just off screen (that is to say, just outside the bounds of this on-screen world, which is interesting precisely because the exact degree of control exercised over it at any point can never be determined) plays an intermittent yet powerful role, marvelously weaving in and out of the interplay of masks, until, finally, in one of the very last sequences, when what is apparently a real fight takes place between two of Warhol's protagonists, the "action" moves off screen altogether for some time. In this connection, we might note that the world of sheer chance (which, as I have said, is usually banished by most film-makers to some forgotten corner of off-screen space) seems to be most palpable when it asserts its presence without ever becoming actually visible, when it lurks just outside the visual field without ever actually entering it, its proximity being somehow conveyed by the sound. As soon as this world of sheer chance erupts on screen, a process of integration begins: This contingent reality (in principle beyond control, in any event uncontrolled), when captured on film, slowly becomes a part of a universe that is somewhat more reassuring, not because of the more realistic nature of sound or the more pronounced stylization of the visual image but simply because of the intrinsically threatening nature of anything invisible and uncontrolled off screen (as any horror film will illustrate). This is particularly true when the film-maker leads us to understand that this lack of control is not at all simulated (as in a horror film) but rather absolutely real, that *anything* in fact can emerge from that off-screen space. In short, when we see images (images that we still usually think of as being controlled by *someone*, whether a director or a cameraman), while at the same time we hear their opposite (that is to say, elements of a noncontrolled universe off screen), the result is a genuinely dialectical tension. Yet as soon as a fragment from the uncontrolled world "enters the scene," bidden or unbidden, it remains a "foreign body" for only a few seconds, losing all its strangeness as gradually this new element (this person) becomes part of whatever is occurring on screen. On the other hand, if a person exits from frame and continues to speak or to make sounds of any kind, he still remains an integral part of the relatively more predictable world of screen space, and in fact extends this world into off-screen space. This, indeed, is one of the great lessons to be learned from *The Chelsea Girls*, suggesting yet another extremely complex parameter simultaneously involving the dialectic of materials, the role assumed by the camera, and the relationship between off-screen space and screen space already discussed.

We now come to Jean-Luc Godard, whose entire body of work from *Une Femme mariée* on essentially depends on the successive roles assumed by the camera (and ultimately the viewer) with regard to the actors and vice versa. In *Une Femme mariée*, alternations between the camera as participant, passive spectator, and "ringmaster" or dictator of the action are rather clearly indicated by Godard: At least whenever the camera is a participant, an inserted numbered title announces the fact just as the extreme stylization of the composition indicates when the camera is the "ringmaster." However, as always happens with Godard (and it is in this connection that the interplay of masks becomes important in his work, too), the actual degree to which the actors were allowed to improvise in other scenes is quite difficult to determine, and because of the important part improvisation plays elsewhere in the film this uncertainty takes on an emphasis that it would not have in the work, say, of a Joseph Mankiewicz.

These ambiguities intervene most systematically in *Deux ou trois choses que je sais d'elle* and, in fact, provide the film with one of its essential underpinnings. The relationship between actor and camera may change at any moment, even in the middle of a shot (as in the brilliant sequence in a fashion boutique where both the salesgirls' and customers' asides are admirably combined in a visual pattern that is almost choreographic in its complexity), or in the middle of a line of dialogue (as in Marina Vlady's monologue at the hairdresser's). At times, the transition is obvious; at times, it becomes evident only after the fact; at times, the exact moment it actually occurs cannot be determined, although the viewer is vaguely aware that "there has been one somewhere."

Godard at times seems to lose sight of the structural and formal (that is, aesthetic) possibilities inherent in this interplay of masks, and in *La Chinoise* these shifts have been reduced at best to their simplest expressive form. Godard's contribution, however, is immense. It is quite possible that without him the principal ideas' underlying this chapter could not have been formulated.

Yet why conceal from the reader my grave misgivings regarding these selfsame "basic ideas?" Often the views expressed seem mere metaphysical abstractions. This chapter is nevertheless perhaps the most important in the book, for even though it may contain but a single truth—the fact that cinematic material is always refractory—this truth is a primary one. Cinematic material is especially refractory to any preconceived ideas we may have of it.[8] Yet are we therefore to reject any and every preconceptual approach to film form and structure, as certain people would have us do? Is the remainder of the book already outdated then? Must cinematic creation become purely empirical? I believe not. I believe that even if this problem has not been dealt with in a convincing manner, it is nevertheless necessary to discover some way of taking the essentially refractory character of this material into account as part of the conceptualization process *preceding* filming. Surely, if a film is to be absolutely rigorous in every respect, the work must take the function of chance into account as early as the *découpage* stage (rather than only during the editing or during location shooting) and must do so both on the level of filmic "texture" (Eisenstein's approach) and on the formal level (*cinéma vérité's* contribution). There seems to be a sort of Heisenbergian uncertainty principle at work between the film-maker and what he films. He cannot aim his camera at anything without modifying it, for what he films, life itself, is irretrievably foreign to the artifices of his instruments. Like modern physicists confronted with certain elementary particles, film-makers therefore must take into account the inevitable gap between their instruments and themselves on the one hand, and life on the other (perhaps by some day combining Eisenstein's approach with Godard's), so as to be able to work on life as a raw material and ultimately shape it, despite this gap, through a work that will thereby be all the richer.

Notes

1. Obviously, the reference here is not to the restricted use of chance in music as a means of choosing between different itineraries for a work, as when Henri Pousseur draws lots.

2. And I feel that it is just as much out of place in literature and the plastic arts, although I have less competence as a critic in these fields.

3. This is a hasty treatment, to say the least, of one of the most important film-makers of the 1920's, whose work was relatively unfamiliar to me at the time and whom I hope to deal with more extensively in a forthcoming book.

4. Nine times out of ten, however, this "realism" is partly destroyed through dubbing and sound-mixing.

5. As the unedited rushes of *Que Viva Mexico* show.

6. The Japanese cinema, on the other hand, particularly during the 1930's, was greatly influenced by the Soviet film-makers, as can be seen not only in the films of Ozu, of course, but also in the works of other directors almost unknown in the West.

7. In *Moi, un noir*, this procedure already exists in rudimentary form, as the characters in that film periodically pretend to be Edward G. Robinson, Lemmy Caution, and Dorothy Lamour.

8. Animated films being in principle the one general exception. However, the case of Norman McLaren is of interest in this regard. In his "best period," the famous Canadian deliberately chose a technique (drawing directly on the film) that introduced a contingent, uncontrollable element into the image, something that had previously been considered a technical defect: namely, the instability of the figures so characteristic of the films McLaren made at that time.

8

Structures of Aggression

In preceding chapters, there have been occasional references to the
feeling of discomfort created by certain types of "match cuts,"
ones that until recently had been considered "bad" matches but
that could be integrated, it was suggested, into a broader, nonnorma-
tive plastic conception of *découpage* wherein the degree and the nature of the resulting discomfort would be taken into account and
regarded as parameters. The discomfort created by disorientation in
particular (because of "bad" eye-line matches, for instance, or "bad"
matches in screen position and direction of movement), the vectors
of which can unquestionably be "controlled," can be handled in
such a way as to result in a new sense of orientation, thus producing
the kind of configuration already described as a "retroactive" or "deferred" match. The important part surprise can play in *découpage*
has likewise been referred to. The end result of a "retroactive" match
is surprise (we are astonished to realize that we were actually
not confronted with the spatial or temporal configuration we
thought we were, just before the transition between shots occurred), and a similar effect is produced by any sudden shift in
awareness of the relationship between screen space and off-screen
space (our surprise, for instance, at realizing that someone was just
outside frame when we thought he was quite a distance away).

Surprise and discomfort as defined here might be said to constitute the two most moderate forms of aggression the film image is capable of inflicting on a viewer; they lie at one end of a whole range of aggressions of increasing intensity and of very different sorts that a film-maker is in a position to practice on his captive audience. This undeniable power tacitly attributed to film-makers from the earliest days of cinema (people instinctively ducked their heads when Lumière's train pulled into the station) soon came to be considered a veritable public menace. The various forms of official or unofficial censorship set up to confront this menace always concentrated on the *content* of the images, naturally, and never on their *form*. But the complaints that have been current in France for some time now[1] with regard to the violent style of certain of the most progressive television film-makers (extremely fast cutting, deliriously paced zooms) lead one to believe that censors may eventually concern themselves with more abstract forms of aggression. Film censorship has always been a means of protecting the mass audience from anything it objected to, from anything that threatened its physical and psychic comfort. Despite certain transient forms of political and social censorship, it is a mistake to view censorship as something arbitrarily imposed on the people by this or that regime. Censorship is, rather, a series of limitations imposed on film-makers by the masses, a gesture of self-defense whereby the masses protect themselves against forms of experience that news commentators refer to as "violent sensations" but that can, of course, consist of a good deal more than that.

The problem of censorship is quite beyond the scope of this book, and the analysis of aesthetic aggression to be undertaken here will be conducted as if censorship were nonexistent, or rather as if it were merely the sociological expression, at a given time and for a given society, of the tension that arises when taboos are violated. The degree to which these taboos are violated is, in fact, precisely the measure of the poetic intensity of the various kinds of aggression about to be described. At a certain level, this conceptual approach has a basis in fact. The dialectic of prohibition and transgression explored by Georges Bataille[2] is to some extent exemplified in the relationships of films to their censors.[3]

I have in fact borrowed the general terms of "transgression" and "prohibition" from Bataille, because all really censurable images, whether erotic, repugnant, violent, or truly subversive (as opposed to images that embarrass a party or a regime, though not society as a whole, and therefore inconvenience a government but do not traumatize its constituents: shots of the slums at Nanterre as opposed to shots of a fraudulent election) are, despite other possible differences, forms of aggression.[4] We will now examine how *pain*—for that is what is involved: most often psychic pain, but sometimes physical pain as well—can be considered to be part of an aesthetic experience when the pain results from some form of dialectical transgression and is experienced by "normal" adults, by persons capable both of bearing up under a dentist's drill without any particular psychic trauma and of apprehending, however vaguely, the abstract dimension of a work of art. *Le Sang des bêtes* is certainly not a film for children, but neither is *Last Year at Marienbad*.[5]

As should be obvious, aggression is thus considered due to the actual content of an image to be basically no different from purely optical aggression (certain films by the great American animator Robert Breer, dizzying cascades of images that "hurt your eyes" come principally to mind)[6] or from more insidious forms of aggression such as those resulting from the kind of disorientation already described.

Every one of these forms of aggression, in fact, has its source in that very special, almost hypnotic relationship that is established between screen and viewer as soon as the lights go down in the theater and that Siegfried Kracauer has analyzed quite well. Whatever his level of critical awareness, a viewer sitting in the dark alone and suddenly face to face with the screen is completely at the mercy of the film-maker, who may do violence to him at any moment and through any means. Should the viewer be forced beyond the pain threshold, his defense mechanisms may well be called forth and he may remind himself that "it's only a movie" (that distancing phenomenon to be described in more detail below), but it will always be too late . . . the harm will already have been done; intense discomfort, and perhaps even terror, will already have crept across the threshold.[7]

The first time any "normal" viewer sees *Un Chien andalou*, the famous shot of the sliced eyeball is experienced as an absolute shock, which is all the more overwhelming because everything prior to it is deliberately intended to lull the viewer's sensibilities, to create a perfectly reassuring mood: a man very contentedly sharpening his razor, smoking, looking at the night from a balcony with a woman quietly sitting at his side. The shot is just as shocking after several viewings of the film, and during a second or subsequent viewing the traumatic power inherent in it sends out a shock wave that reaches right back to the beginning of the film, so that the "flat" opening sequence takes on the most bizarre sort of emotional shading in anticipation. *Un Chien andalou* was to my knowledge the first film in the history of cinema to have attempted to use aggression as one of its structural components. The presence of a shock wave simultaneously propagating itself both backward and forward from an image that is the film's undeniable center of gravity, its pre-eminently privileged moment, undoubtedly has as much to do with form as with the creation of a dreamlike atmosphere. After roughly two minutes' running time, this crucial shot appears, the effect of which is to divide the film into two separate parts. At the same time, each of the two parts takes on a poetic meaning radically different from the one it would have possessed had there been no such shot. As proof of this, I need only point out that there exists a bowdlerized version in which this close-up of the eye is missing and that it produces on anyone acquainted with the complete version the same effect as does a black-and-white print of a film previously seen in color.

Despite the capital interest of *Un Chien andalou*, aggression has since been used only rarely in this intense a form as a structural element (see, however, the opening of Buñuel's *Land Without Bread* with its gradual progression from the banal to the horrifying). Were it not for Georges Franju's masterpiece *Le Sang des bêtes* (1949), *Un Chien andalou* would appear to have led to a dead end.

The manner in which Franju's short film opens presents a number of striking analogies with the opening of the film by Dali and Buñuel. The images full of a "populist" poetry, accompanied by sentimental music and a nostalgic narration, lull the viewer, thus performing much the same function as the night sky in *Un Chien andalou*. Once again we have no idea that misfortune awaits us. Were it not for the title of the film, we would be as trusting as the nice horse we see being gently led through the courtyard of the slaughterhouse. Even when a small tube is placed over the horse's muzzle, the whole situation seems too ordinary, too humdrum for there to be any sense of impending doom. A sharp detonation follows and the animal pitches over as if struck by lightning, an image of sudden death more overwhelming, perhaps, than any other previously seen in film[8] because of its stark simplicity. The viewer has undergone his first shock. In contrast to what occurs in *Un Chien andalou*, this shock is repeated with endless variations throughout the film. The entire rhythm of the work is based on a succession of painful shocks felt as directly as the electrical charges once administered to viewers sitting in wired seats by rather naïve exponents of "total cinema" during the showing of certain horror films in the United States. Rhythm seems to be the appropriate term, for these shocks are quite varied in intensity and sometimes are separated by documentary or lyrical sequences of varying length, while at other times they occur in extremely close proximity, as when some ten lambs are slaughtered in the span of a few seconds and their dead bodies then inflated with compressed air and skinned, this being followed by a prolonged shot showing the steaming carcasses, a kind of *fioritura* of an astonishing beauty that nonetheless seems to emit the very smell of death. The somewhat facile black humor coloring certain sequences occasionally mars the purity of the film's structures, particularly in the scene where a butcher "splits his steer as the clock strikes twelve," yet these structures exist, created principally by the editing and the admirable sound effects contributed by Jean Painlevé. Most importantly, from the point of view that concerns us here, they are structures whose very substance is horror, and they are inevitably perceived (except by persons of extremely perverse sensibility) through a cloud of pain. Beyond the humanitarian or vegetarian concerns that may perhaps motivate certain more sensitive souls, each of us is vulnerable to these brutal assaults on bodies that, after all, are terrifyingly similar to our own. What makes the image of the slit eyeball in *Un Chien andalou* so painful if not the realization of our own eyes' vulnerability to the slash of a razor? *Le Sang des bêtes*, in short, undeniably presents us with an almost musical interaction between moments of tension and moments of respite, in the form of more or less closely spaced and more or less pronounced crossings of the pain threshold.

But, in this respect, *Le Sang des bêtes* remains the only film of its kind. In the United States, where the limits set by censorship have receded considerably over these last few years, films have been made that in actual fact are little more than sexual fantasies of human slaughter (*Blood Feast, Two Thousand Maniacs*). It is rather doubtful that the directors of these movies had the sense of form that Franju possessed when he was making his first short films, or that form has any more than an accidental function in their work. These films are nonetheless interesting works, in so far as the traumatic power inherent in their images undoubtedly provides raw material that other film-makers more sensitive to the complexities of form and more conscious of contemporary formal methods could exploit. Aside from the question of censorship, are film-makers in the West willing or able to exploit material of this sort? Generally speaking, the European film-makers most concerned with problems of form— Bresson, Antonioni, Resnais[9]—tend to exclude from their work any painful violations of taboos, or include such violations only reluctantly, inserting any such element in their films in the most gingerly sort of way (the sex in Resnais's *La Guerre est finie*, the violent fights in Bresson's *Au Hasard Balthazar*). On the other hand, when Buñuel rather late in his career becomes conscious of form in the sense in which the word is used here, in works as accomplished as *Diary of a Chambermaid* and *Belle de jour*, he suddenly acquires a sense of modesty; his images are no longer as corrosive as they were in works such as *Los Olvidados* and *El*—less accomplished works, it might be added.

The Japanese, however, are more accustomed to living with their fears: The modern individual probably fears death just as much as his Western counterpart, but Japanese society as a whole seems to have better assimilated the idea of death. Like Franju's great documentary, the Japanese fiction film offers a whole tradition of cruelty in Antonin Artaud's sense of the word, whose specifically structural potential has been sensed by more than a few film-makers.[10] Akira Kurosawa's masterpiece, *Throne of Blood*, is built around a central alternation between scenes of extreme agitation and scenes of an almost unbearably tense quiescence, the most striking of which is an extremely prolonged shot of Asaji ("Lady Macbeth") waiting for her husband, Washizu, to kill their lord. Yet neither this murder nor any of the other violence (war, murders, etc.) in the "story" takes place on screen: A battle scene is *represented* by furious gallopings about far behind the actual front, and Washizu's killing of the assassin is a stylized gesture seen in a very "undramatic" long shot. It is only in the final scene in which thousands of arrows pierce Washizu's body as he dashes along the ramparts of his castle, that the on-screen agitation and hitherto off-screen violence are finally united in images that constitute a kind of "coda" that is both disruptive and recapitulative, releasing as it does the tension built up previously by the evacuation of violence from the screen.

A strikingly similar example of a dialectics of horror may be cited in the work of a less prestigious but very prolific director, Shiro Toyada. His film *Japanese Ghosts* is built around alternations of images that are extremely suggestive in their understatement and others possessed of a very crude sort of horror, these alternations generally involving the same element. A scene in which a bandit kills an old man in the forest is a good example. The fatal blow is barely visible and the body topples over out of camera range. The murderer then leans over the invisible body and performs some vague sort of laborious task; perhaps he is stripping the body of a purse attached to the victim's waist or hanging around his neck. A second bandit appears on the scene and the first bandit tells him of his evil deed, adding that he has peeled the skin off the old man's face so that his victim will be unrecognizable! Fair enough . . . the film-maker's approach seems obvious: horror by suggestion. (This use of off-screen space is a case of "deferred apprehension".) Then two absolutely horrifying shots in rapid succession bluntly show us what has thus far been so carefully concealed, the flayed head on the ground, followed by an image of fierce beauty, the skin of the face hanging in one piece from a small tree. An undeniable formal structure—a kind of reduction of the over-all form of *Throne of Blood*—is involved here; moreover, it is used several times without losing any of its effectiveness. We have difficulty adjusting to the horrifying, and the structure has its *raison d'être* in that mixture of repugnance and fascination experienced by the viewer confronted with these images of horror. He is titillated at first by the suggested horror and thinks he has gotten off easily with a little shiver running up his spine, but then suddenly absolutely everything is revealed to him! This "Chinese-box" technique is rich in formal possibilities. Within a register somewhat below the pain threshold, certain American gangster films take violence as the basic material, dealing with it through a technique that we might call, using a musical analogy, "variations on a theme"; Richard Wilson's *Al Capone* is, in fact, conceived as a series of variations on the theme of murder by surprise, each murder being carried out in a more baroque and unpredictable manner than the one before. The film, however, is a typical Hollywood product—that is to say, one with only a very slight formal awareness; structures of this sort can at best be regarded here as fortunate accidents resulting from commercial practicality.

It would be quite unfair to say the same about the masterpieces of the golden age of American slapstick, a cinematic form based, on the one hand, on obvious forms of aggression, and, on the other, on visible structures. In Mack Sennett's, Buster Keaton's, Harry Langdon's, and especially Laurel and Hardy's best films, structure and aggression almost always go hand in hand. The aggression can occur in a great variety of forms and intensities. Surprise, an essential cause of laughter (as Georges Bataille has put it, "the unknown makes us laugh") is also involved, of course, usually occurring in conjunction with deferred structures of an extremely amusing sort.

One of the most beautiful moments in *Sherlock Junior* is surely the scene in which Keaton, before entering the outlaws' hideout, affixes some kind of hoop covered with paper to the outside of one of the windows of the shack. Once inside, as soon as the bandits become menacing, Keaton does a magnificent dive through the window and the hoop, which turns out to have an old woman's disguise hidden inside it, which Keaton is decked out in even before hitting the ground. As he hobbles off, the bandits burst out the door, quite perplexed at seeing that their quarry has escaped them with such incredible speed, for naturally they pay no attention to the old woman.

We are at once outraged and amazed at this surprising and improbable gimmick, and our laughter is a response to this mild aggression. At the same time, the *beauty* of the sequence derives from its structure. Keaton prepares the window, enters through the door, and dives through the window as the outlaws come out the door; our initial perplexity at Keaton's preparations is the counterpart of the outlaws' confusion when they confront the result of the preparations, and so on. James Agee, among others, has analyzed the gags of this period in this way. But it should be particularly emphasized that the beauty of the structure is experienced through laughter provoked by aggression, in exactly the same way that the beauty of the rhythm underlying *Le Sang des bêtes* is apprehended through the pain created by an aggression of an altogether different kind. However, the laughter caused by the great American slapstick artists is not always as unmixed as it is here, at least not for the sensitive adult. The aggression sometimes comes a good deal closer to crossing the pain threshold. Harold Lloyd dangling over the ledge of a skyscraper is an image out of a nightmare; laughter and terror mingle, giving a very special coloration to some admirably structured acrobatics. And, when Laurel and Hardy in one of those "proliferating" structures that were their own special secret, demolish a whole line of cars, make scores of people double up in pain on the sidewalk by punching them in the solar plexus, or push a whole crowd of people into a mud puddle (scatalogical aggression such as this is extremely common in slapstick films), the viewer feels that he is the direct victim of a *structured aggression*, and his somewhat strained laughter is accompanied by a very pure aesthetic satisfaction. A final altogether admirable example is provided by the sequence in *Long Pants* in which Harry Langdon, after having daydreamed of murdering his fiancée so he can run away with a gangster's vamp, attempts to act out his fantasy. When he asks the ingenuous girl a second time whether she wants to "take a walk in the woods" while attempting at the same time to hide an enormous Army revolver in his pocket, literally repeating a shot previously seen in his daydream, the result is one of the most outrageous surprise gags of the period. And the interminable scene that follows (during which he desperately attempts to distract his fiancée's attention long enough to be able to kill her from a distance exactly as the whole thing has taken place in his fantasy) provides an extraordinary example of variations on a theme occurring within an atmosphere of slapstick nightmare that soon becomes unbearable. Once again acute anxiety mingles with laughter and this ambiguous aggression develops within a formal pattern (the ideal event being established in the daydream, followed by frantic variations on it brought on by all the obstacles that come up in reality) that is almost mathematical in its rigor.

Unfortunately today, the art of slapstick seems dead and buried. It constitutes a genre indissolubly linked with a period of American history[11] that represents the only major collective contribution made by the American movie industry to the art of film, comparable to the contribution made by the French primitives and the German expressionists, and perhaps even comparable to that of the great Soviet experimenters. Until relatively recently, however, the best elements of slapstick survived in a certain tendency of the American animated cartoon, first in Walt Disney's work then, after his decline, in the work of that master of the delirious, Tex Avery. As Georges Sadoul wrote of Avery: "The free play of his imagination, the almost surrealistic gags, the grating humor, the sardonic ferocity evident in the small number of films he made based on a chase and a battle to the death, all to a strange syncopated rhythm, revolutionized the animated cartoon." Avery, who seems to have remained completely inactive after Warner Brothers closed down their animation studios, possessed a sense of excess in everything and of its organization, which distinguish his films from the stereotyped frenzy characteristic of the majority of American cartoons. Two characters hurtle off a cliff uttering horrendous screams; during shot after shot they fall toward the camera and their repeated cries finally become unbearable; the scene lasts for only about ten seconds but appears to go on forever. Then they finally land, as light as feathers, and the chase resumes as if nothing had happened. Elsewhere in the same film (the title of which unfortunately does not come to mind) the Cat hides inside a hollow tree trunk, and the Dog, believing he's finally cornered him, slips his paw into the hole only to grab hold of a tomato held out by the Cat. The Dog squeezes it fiercely and pulls his paw out, smeared with red. Then in one of those crazy reversals, one of those delirious breaks in tone characteristic of Avery's work, the Dog starts to moan, "I crushed him! I crushed him!" and his lamentations go on and on, to the point where we actually feel uncomfortable, and the scene is no longer funny. The moment when the Cat reappears and the chase goes on is almost a relief.

We have now come full circle. Having started with the discomfort created by "bad" matches, we have now arrived at the discomfort resulting from the grating humor underlying Tex Avery's syncopated rhythms. These two forms of malaise are perhaps not as foreign to each other as might initially be imagined. The creation of discomfort as a form of aggression is becoming more and more important in the thematic material of contemporary cinema. One of the most striking recent examples of discomfort created through aggression, a film certain to arouse heated controversy, is Marcel Hanoun's *L'Authentique procès de Carl Emmanuel Jung*. Based on material dealing with the horrible happenings in Nazi extermination camps, the work uses an imaginary trial as a pretext and is filmed in the most stylized manner conceivable (there is no courtroom set; the actors are simply filmed separately against a dark background and confront each other only through the editing). The voices of the actors who are giving testimony about the events in the camps with restrained but obviously intense emotion are never actually heard. The text is spoken for them by the mechanical, neutral, unsynchronized voices of translators, and this distancing already creates a certain uneasiness. What is more, the very subject of the film, represented by the contrast between the gruesome testimony at the trial and the glimpses of the peaceful family life of the fifty-year-old man we are told was a cruel torturer twenty-five years earlier, is naturally one that is highly disturbing to everyone. And finally, both the plastic form and the visual style of the film (in every respect, worthy of the maker of *Une Simple histoire*, even if the style has become more sober) develop quite independently of the horrifying nature of the testimony, sometimes even taking the form of a completely gratuituous visual fantasy, and thus constitute a third source of uneasiness. This discomfort reaches a climax near the end of the film when, after some particularly detailed testimony concerning the conditions inside the gas chambers, a particularly "artistic" succession of shots occurs, showing a nude girl twisting and turning on an unmade bed. The shot has already been seen several times and seems strikingly gratuitous, for nothing in the spare comments of the newspaperman (one of the characters in the film) provides any explanation for it. After several seconds have gone by, the reporter's voice is heard, obviously speaking to the woman he loves (who is clearly the girl on the screen, although she has not previously been referred to), describing a nightmare he has had: He has dreamed that she was one of the Nazi executioners' victims and was dragging herself naked across the floor of the gas chamber. In this particular case the "distance effect" resulting from the viewer's discomfort, on the one hand, and the manner in which the structure has developed in time (through the premonitory shots) and space (organization of matches and frame compositions), on the other, works perfectly. The effect produced, at once disturbing and very moving, could never have been attained without the temporal development, and the almost too meticulously perfect spatial relationships are only beautiful relative to the feeling of discomfort, which controverts our aesthetic pleasure and suddenly makes their beauty horrible.

It is probable that there will be well-meaning viewers who will violently object to Hanoun's film on the grounds that no one has the right to consider the suffering and death of millions of Jews as an aesthetic object, for that in my view is Hanoun's approach in this very beautiful film. There is no intention here of deciding this serious question one way or another. It can only be noted in passing that numerous creative artists, among them many who are far from second-rate, have made evil into an object of beauty, generally through erotic fantasy. (Sade, Genet, Lautréamont, Bataille, and, in cinema, Leni Riefenstahl come to mind.) Those who refuse to accept this attitude (or reject it in cinema, which amounts to the same thing) and therefore reject Hanoun's approach, which is a good deal more restrained and also more ambiguous, are the same people who —for perfectly understandable reasons—are often incapable of regarding Nazi extermination camps and other more recent horrors as part of the "drama of history." But surely every creator has the right to use this "drama" as a source of inspiration and treat it however he pleases. This attitude toward Hanoun is no different from that which led a certain dilettantish leftist critic to accuse Ingmar Bergman of political opportunism for having included a series of shots from a Vietnam newsreel in *Persona*. This critic is so blinded by his own system of values that he does not see that to a mind like Bergman's the sight of a Buddhist monk setting himself on fire is no longer an image with a political meaning, but an image of human violence and injustice, and therefore a poetic element that was necessary at that precise moment in the film. Bergman the man may very well thoroughly disapprove of American policy and its application in Vietnam, but that has to do with politics—that is, with life—and if ever there was a film-maker who clearly let it be understood that for him art and life are two separate entities it is Bergman. Is it that surprising that Bergman is not Godard?[12]

Indeed, one of my aims when writing this chapter was the rehabilitation of taboo materials (often with no other connection between them except the fact that they are taboo), which is both possible and desirable in the light of the particular concept of structure defined throughout this book. As a matter of fact, the other goal in this chapter was to demonstrate, through the example of violence and aggression in all their forms, that even those materials apparently most resistant to the "mathematics of form" and the most highly charged emotionally can be "sublimated" through formal abstraction and still retain their full emotional impact. As Pierre Boulez has put it, "For delirium to become an effective creative factor, it must be taken into account and organized."

Notes

1. In 1967. French television has become considerably more tame since then . . . in every conceivable way.
2. Bataille, however, was not particularly concerned with the abstractions of form, and to my knowledge never derived conclusions of a structural sort from this dialectic.
3. Necessarily in an incoherent form, for in an area as subjective as this it is a good deal more difficult for a group of men to express the desires of society as a whole than in other areas.
4. A hurried reading of the above might give the impression that I am defending censorship. That is definitely not true. Censorship for adults, either for supposedly good reasons or for bad ones, must be fought by every film-maker and film-lover in every possible way. Unfortunately, this is far from always being the case. Film censorship exists in some form or other in every country; the universality of the phenomenon should make us realize that it stems from the very nature of the medium and therefore has aesthetic as well as political consequences that every film-maker should be aware of.
5. American children are permitted to see the most gruesome horror films. Not that horror films of this sort are responsible for American juvenile delinquency; rather, the violence inherent in American life gives children in that country a sophisticated awareness that prepares them for these films. Some psychiatrists believe that such movies, in fact, are excellent cathartic devices permitting children and even certain adults to project their fantasies of aggression without harming themselves or others. In Europe, on the other hand, there is some justification for prohibiting young children from at-

tending certain films (as against banning these entirely), for the European child living in a society where daily violence is rare, is far more sheltered, and therefore more vulnerable than his American counterpart.

6. Today, of course, the "flicker" film is a well-known area of experimentation.

7. It should nevertheless be pointed out that in actual practice this bondage of the viewer has rarely been used for purposes as "noble" as those singled out for attention here. And, considering the part it plays in the alienating function of illusionist, "degree-zero" cinema, it is very important to distinguish between the "good" and "bad" uses of the participative phenomenon (a good use, as implicitly defined here, being dialectical "identification" tempered by "distanciation").

8. A comparable example in the fiction film is Nana's death in *Vivre sa vie*. The role of violence is always quite complex and varies in each of Godard's films, and it deserves a separate study.

9. Ingmar Bergman is the exception proving the rule. His case, however, is a rather complex one that will be touched on below.

10. Recently in Europe we have come to know the film-makers of the post-Kurosawa generation, many of whom are directly concerned with the aesthetic use of violence (see in particular Oshima, Wakamatsu, Yoshida, and above all, perhaps, Matsumoto, whose *Shura* [1972], a neo-Brechtian reworking of a Kabuki drama makes systematic use of extreme violence as both a structural and distancing device). It goes without saying that Western censors, particularly in Europe, keep most of the films containing similar material from the public screen.

11. The contribution made in France by Jean Durand, who at least in his use of aggression has no peer (as in *Zigoto, plombier*, where an entire building is demolished by a clumsily handled ladder, or in *Zigoto, détective*, where a decrepit, old housemaid is brutally knocked unconscious by the Herculean hero) should not be overlooked, however.

12. Written at a time when my views on the ideological implications of artistic practice were confused to say the least, this paragraph is from my present viewpoint very naïve pleading for a badly defined cause. Rather than delete or rewrite it, I have preferred to leave it as specific testimony to the intellectual confusion that explains many of the book's inadequacies.

IV

Reflections on the Film Subject

9

Fictional Subjects

Having started from an area of investigation so circumscribed, so modest, so rudimentary that no one seems to have concerned himself with it in a systematic manner before, we have reached a point as we near the end of this work where I can discuss another realm so vast and "noble" that almost all film criticism has been devoted to it. Even in *Les Cahiers du cinéma*, over three-quarters of the articles published are chiefly concerned with a film's subject, and when problems of film form and film syntax are touched upon it is invariably from this point of view. If, after so much ink has flowed, I nonetheless venture out into such thoroughly explored territory, if I nonetheless reserve a prominent place in this book for a treatment of the film subject, it is because my approach is diametrically opposed to that of all critics and nearly all film theoreticians and historians (though not that of certain film-makers). On the one hand, the film subject will be dealt with in terms of problems of form and discourse, an approach consistent with the over-all attitude toward cinema expressed in this book. On the other hand, and more importantly, I intend to approach the subject as a generic term, whereas ordinarily it is approached as the sum total of specific cases, as a series of subjects.

If one is willing to concede that film has at least partially discovered its inherent structural possibilities and that this fact should be taken into account when the moment comes to choose a film's subject, one necessarily has to ask oneself what a film subject *is*, or rather, what constitutes a "good" film subject, or more accurately still, what a "good" film subject is *today*.

Except for the great so-called primitives (Georges Méliès, Émile Cohl, Louis Feuillade) and some of the great slapstick directors of the early days of the cinema, in whose work the subject fulfilled a certain formal function, traditional film-makers have tended to adopt one or the other of the following two attitudes toward the film subject: Either they have held that only the subject mattered and the manner in which it was handled was important in so far as it enhanced the "content," a position held by most "quality" commercial directors, of whom Claude Autant-Lara provides a good example; or, conversely, they have maintained that the film's subject was not at all important, that only the manner in which it was treated mattered; it is the position not only of a minor artist like Henri-Georges Clouzot, but of a director as important as Sternberg. Paradoxically enough, these two seemingly opposite attitudes reflected a single idea, one that present-day conceptions have begun to refute, namely, that a film-maker is merely a director, someone who takes a script of his own or someone else's creation, which he then renders into images. André S. Labarthe has quite succinctly described this quarrel of vocabulary—which is also a conflict of generations—and shown how this dichotomy conceals a very serious underlying problem:

> Of the twin concepts that allow criticism to "grasp" films (as a lobster claw might), *mise-en-scène* bypasses the subject, so to speak, and refers to its *rendering*. From [Louis] Delluc on, judging a film always involved judging the acting, the quality of the dialogue, the beauty of the photography, the effectiveness of the editing . . . and if, for some thirty or forty years, film criticism has more or less managed to "grasp" its object, it is simply because cinema has barely evolved at all, or rather has evolved only within the limits set by the notion of *mise-en-scène*.[1]

When Sternberg made *The Scarlet Empress*, he was quite aware that his screen play was an insignificant trifle. What was important to him was creating a visual object, and, to fulfill that goal, he had to undertake an operation that in effect involved *putting things into images*, as one might put ships into bottles or pictures on pages. Although Autant-Lara (in films such as *Devil in the Flesh* and *La Traversée de Paris*) was led to create a style as artificial as Sternberg's, it was precisely for the opposite reason: He wanted it to *serve the subject*, which to him was of primary importance. For Sternberg, *mise-en-scène* is an end in itself; for Autant-Lara, it is only a means. The relative importance assigned style and content by the two directors is reversed, but their underlying concept of film is in the last analysis identical: Both believe that there is some hierarchical relationship between a film's subject and its form (or in their words a film's "style"). Other well-intentioned people in the film world frequently refer to a "fusion of form and content," but this merely represents another posture based on aesthetic views that have been outdated for a century now, for these advocates of a "great synthesis" still consider the writing of a scenario and its plastic elaboration as two separate and distinct stages, thereby necessarily implying some form of priority between them. Each view, in fact, sees a film's *découpage* as essentially a process giving visual form to a previously existing content, and, no matter how transcendent this process is to some film-makers and how subservient it is to a film's content to others, it is always performed *after the fact*, is always superimposed upon a pre-existing screen play, which in itself is the *literary* development of a subject of some sort or other.

Obviously there have been exceptions. One of the most significant of these in the period between World War I and World War II is undoubtedly Renoir's *La Règle du jeu*—a masterpiece largely for this very reason. If *La Règle du jeu* is one of the first truly modern films, it is because Renoir chose the subject matter precisely for the interesting formal problems it raised and because the form and even the texture of the film derive *directly* from its subject matter. Therein lies the key to the problem of the film subject in a contemporary context. When film-makers finally become fully conscious of the cinematic means at their disposal, when the possibility of creating organically coherent films in which every element works with every other is within sight, surely the subject matter of a film, the element that is almost always the starting point of the process of making a film, must be conceived in terms of its ultimate form and texture. That at least seems to be a proper contemporary formulation of the problem. Renoir already saw this very clearly when he chose the subject matter of *La Règle du jeu*, as he himself proved by the very relevant comments he made in his conversations with Jacques Rivette in one of the *Cinéastes de notre temps* television series. To state what should be obvious, the mad chases back and forth, the continual comings and goings of all sorts that bring the depth of field and off-screen space into play in a very complex way and constitute the essential formal devices of *La Règle du jeu*, are merely the literal extension (the "augmentation," as musicians would say) of the mistaken identities of lovers and the mutual meddlings of servants and masters in each other's worlds, which provide the film with its content. Even taking the term in its simplest sense, the subject is contained in microcosm not only in each sequence but in almost every shot, on a certain level of analysis at least.

It might perhaps be better to describe how a subject can engender form by briefly comparing two minor films by a director whose formal concerns, although constant, are somewhat more superficial than Renoir's and therefore provide a clearer example: Alfred Hitchcock's *Rope* and *The Birds*, two of the best films from his American period. *Rope* is based on a subject much like that of a classical theatrical melodrama, with the traditional three acts, dramatic entrances and exits, and so on. The actual visual form of the film, however, results from an arbitrary decision, the elimination of the cut. On a poetic level, perhaps, this formal decision is in perfect accord with the subject of the film, but in no sense can the form be said to derive from the subject matter. An altogether different approach is used in *The Birds*. Here the entire structure, even the actual style of the film is implicit in the subject itself, the gradual destruction of the American dream, of the sterile and comfortable fantasies of middle-class life as Hollywood depicts it. Starting with the first peck of a bird's beak on Tippi Hedren's forehead, middle-class reality is progressively contaminated by violence; the film's entire development is based on this spread of violence, which underlies both the individual images and the over-all *découpage*. The film, like the subject on which it is based, has a beginning, but it does not have an end, or, if it does, it is buried under the millions of birds that have invaded the screen (the world). *The Birds* is a film in which everything *at every level* derives directly from the premise laid down by the basic plot.

In this cellular relationship between the subject matter and the way in which it is rendered, we discover another analogy, a particularly rewarding one, between contemporary film forms and the strategies of contemporary music. Serial composers appear to us to have a very similar conception of the relationships between the basic choice of a tone row or tone rows (which provides a musical work with its "subject," what classical musicians called the "theme" of a work, although tone rows function quite differently) and the form of the finished work. Serial composers believe that the entire development of a musical work must be derived from the basic cell or at least be located relative to it, even if the actual cellular unit is never recognizable as such.

To serial composers, the almost biological growth of a musical work from a few generating cells, a conception that originated in the great works of Debussy and Schoenberg, is only part of a broader attempt to endow a musical work with a greater and greater organic coherence.[2] With similar ends in view, certain film-makers have recently begun to concentrate on establishing relationships of the same order between the subjects they choose to film and the final style and structure of the films derived from these subjects.

We have already examined at some length two films, *Cronaca di un amore* and *Une Simple histoire*, which represent, each in its own way, important stages on the way to a definition of the structural function of the subject. Rather than repeat what was already said, the reader is referred to Chapter 6, which can be reread in the light of the remarks that follow.

But first a very necessary parenthesis. Among film-makers, there might seem to be little need to provide a definition of a "film subject," particularly with regard to the fiction film—a film, that is, based on a fictional dramatic narrative. Any film-maker recognizes as film subjects the short summaries he can read any week under the heading "New Films" in the entertainment section of the paper.

However, a contemporary writer might view such items with a certain scorn, as being mere "résumés of the plot." Whereas writers are becoming more and more deeply interested in transcendent phenomena, a film-maker, because of the very material nature of his art, a materiality as great as that of sculpture for instance, must attach himself to the concrete, to *immanent* realities. Thus, for film-makers, the "subject" of Witold Gombrowicz's great modern novel *Cosmos* is not at all "interpretation considered as an approach to the universe" or any other abstract statement, but simply "two men enter into the life of a household in which certain mysterious signs lead them to conclude that some enigma exists, which they then attempt to resolve . . . or to embody." Obviously, it is quite possible that Gombrowicz himself took purely abstract problems as his point of departure, but this abstraction is of no use to the film-maker involved in the task of making the novel into a film; what would interest him would be the concrete visual structures, the theme of the hanging object, the interchanges of roles, and so on. Film is made first of all out of images and sounds; ideas intervene (perhaps) later. At least this is true in the "fiction film." But, as we shall see in the next chapter, for some years now a nonfiction cinema has existed, whose *point of departure* is the interaction of abstract ideas considered as the "subject," and whose final result is that combination of images and sounds known as a film. But let us go back now to the attempt to define the film subject.

One of the most important steps toward a functionalization of the subject is the work of Alain Robbe-Grillet—in his novels as well as his films. His novels constitute an altogether original attempt at "written cinema," although initially this notion of "written cinema" was a bit puerile. Faced with the obvious exhaustion of traditional novel forms, Robbe-Grillet in *The Erasers* rather naïvely employed all sorts of pseudo-cinematic techniques (dissolves, tracking shots, pans, close-ups, and so on). In the novels published after *The Erasers*, long descriptions, so detailed as to border on parody, have contributed to creating what was has been scornfully called "a land-surveyor's aesthetic." He was apparently attempting thereby to create a literary equivalent of the concreteness and "objective" precision *naturally* characteristic of the film image. This aspect of his experimental novels is what has principally attracted the attention of many young writers, although it is really of secondary importance. Be that as it may, as a film-maker Robbe-Grillet obviously has not pursued this line of research. Although his attempt to catalogue objects in his work has no doubt left its mark on the history of literature, it is rather improbable that it will have much effect on the history of cinema.

Robbe-Grillet's contribution to a new definition of the interaction between subject and form is of incalculable importance however. It is probable that his work will have its most far-reaching consequences in film, for, when applied to literature, the techniques he employs run the risk of becoming tedious because of the essential monotony of the printed word as it lies on the page, whereas in film the same techniques can affect a whole range of material on every level. The theme-and-variations principle he introduced into the art of narrative assumes infinitely more substantial possibilities when applied to the composite art of cinema. No doubt, it is for that very reason that this creative artist has devoted himself to film-making with an enthusiasm that is unprecedented among men of letters of his stature.

We might best begin a brief examination of Robbe-Grillet's contribution with a rather simple example, his second novel, *The Voyeur*. The book's plot (what we call the subject) develops in a relatively continuous manner, broken in the middle however by a long time-ellipsis in which the only real action of the novel, a murder, occurs. A continuous development interrupted by some sort of "jump" or abridgement can be found at every level of the narrative, from a single sentence to the entire novel, including every intermediary phase. This is why his novels are so important for film-makers. He creates a proliferating narrative that grows like a crystal from a basic "cell" to form an entity that is completely coherent even in its contradictions, for every one of its facets reflects in a more or less recognizable form the seminal idea in which the whole originated. No novel of the nineteenth-century type could have the formal unity possessed by one of Robbe-Grillet's works, even the least successful of them. If (as it surely can) film, like music, can gain something from progressing toward greater and greater organic unity, the narrative forms that literature so generously furnished film over the last forty years obviously are no longer of any use. The subjects underlying these old narrative forms, however, can still be of some service, provided the film-maker deduces strictly *cinematic* formal and structural consequences from them. If logically deduced, these consequences will result in a cinematic development of the subject radically different from the literary development the same subject might have led to, as can be seen by comparing Musset's *Les Caprices de Marianne* with Renoir's *La Règle du jeu*.

In his first screen play to be made into a film, *Last Year at Marien-bad*, Robbe-Grillet took this concern for organic unity even further than in *The Voyeur*. Each shot, each incident, refers the viewer to at least one other moment and usually several other moments in the film through repetition, variation, or contradiction; precisely by appealing to the viewer's memory, by testing the viewer's recollection of the preceding details of the film as it unfolds before him, Robbe-Grillet and Resnais have created a work that reflects its subject in miniature at every moment, a subject that can be summarized, although not adequately described, as "three people's completely different recollections of the same event." This progressive thematic unity is what allows us to follow the extraordinary variety of inter-woven threads linking every shot to every other, thus reinforcing the linear movement created by the editing. It is unfortunate, however, that the *découpage* and editing of *Marienbad* do not participate more frequently in the creation of this network of interrelationships, which stem principally from the drama being unfolded, from the actual *content* of the images. The "camera" is perhaps too content merely weaving arabesques around the events, thereby failing to create the sort of genuinely *dialectical* relationship between partici-pation and nonparticipation in the action that underlies *Cronaca di un amore*. In this respect, *Marienbad* also seems perhaps less success-ful than *Une Simple histoire*. Only certain sequences such as those in the continually transformed bedroom and out on the terrace are really tightly articulated. However, reservations of this sort are of no great moment in the light of the extraordinary step forward *Marien-bad* represents in the history of film, particularly with regard to the reintegration of the film subject into the very texture of a work.

The same holds true, moreover, for Robbe-Grillet's first film as a director, *L'Immortelle*, though at the time of its release I (and a good number of my friends) unfortunately underestimated its im-portance by virtue of a too hasty comparison with the visual opu-lence of *Marienbad*. On the material, textural level, it is true, Michel Fano's sound track is the only really functional element in what at the time was an attempt at a brand new type of unity; however, we were doubtless wrong to be disappointed in the film, for how could a com-pletely inexperienced film-maker have been expected to create a totally coherent work when so few film-makers with more experience have done so? But looking back on *L'Immortelle* today, the film seems to me to be a complete success from the standpoint of what Louis Delluc meant by *découpage*—the succession of events, scenes, and even individual shots as "containers" or units of meaning. *L'Immortelle's* "program"—a term that we cannot perhaps substitute for "subject" but one that nonetheless singularly clarifies Robbe-Grillet's approach —consists of a gradual deterioration in verisimilitude, accomplished through a labyrinthine series of coincidences that become more and more fortuitous. This progression exists on every level of the film, in entire scenes as well as in individual shots. As the film unfolds, there are more and more sequences and even individual shots in which there is a progression from an apparently coherent reality to an increasingly pronounced, frozen artificiality as the hero confronts a series of coincidences and contradictions, a formal development perfectly reflecting the narrative progression from an atmosphere of deliberate banality toward an "unacceptable" artifice, a series of supernatural coincidences right out of a H. P. Lovecraft novel. And indeed, this intrusion of "impossible" mysteries into everyday reality has its source in the fantastic novel. But what is important here is that Robbe-Grillet has used it both as a principle of narrative form and of plastic composition—another great step toward the total unity of film.

It is commonly agreed that the subjects of *Marienbad* and *L'Immortelle* are "obscure," but that attitude stems from a grave confusion in terms that merits discussion. The subject of *Marienbad* is obscure only if one persists in believing that the action occurring on screen has a single underlying truth that explains everything, only if one persists in believing, that is to say, that every film possesses a key allowing one to resolve the various contradictions, to opt for what A says rather than what X says, to decide that a given shot has to do with fantasy while another shot has to do with reality. As those responsible for the film have repeatedly said, *Marienbad* has no key. The verbal or visual contradictions are the very essence of the work; they do not conceal the subject, but rather are directly derived from it and furnish yet another example of how this subject is the crucial factor in the film's entire development. In certain respects, both *Marienbad* and *L'Immortelle* are "innocent" films; nothing remains hidden, nothing that is not immediately perceptible in the film exists "somewhere else," above all not in the creators' minds. They are not films that call for interpretation; they demand simply to be seen. In every sense they are films that must be approached naïvely. There is nothing that will do more to spoil the pleasure we should experience by allowing ourselves to become lost in these labyrinths constructed to intrigue our minds and our eyes than the search for a hidden meaning "behind" them.

Hidden meanings, of course, can always be detected; hundreds, thousands of them can be found in these films if the viewer is so inclined. Yet Mack Sennett and Louis Feuillade showed us long ago that great cinema can be a purely immediate experience, and, as paradoxical as it might seem, films such as *Marienbad* and *L'Immortelle* continue that noble tradition. This is simply another way of saying that the subject in its most seminal definition is only a résumé of the action, even if the action in this case is purely mental.

Films that for one reason or another can be described as obscure obviously exist, however—films, that is to say, with a more or less hidden subject. We might ask at this point what the function of such subjects is and how films based on them should be "read."

Without attempting to draw up an exhaustive list of every possible kind of obscure film, one can immediately distinguish several important types. On the one hand, there are films that conceal a simple subject by "going beyond" it, surrounding it with digressions that act as a sort of mask, one that may at times have very elaborate Byzantine contours, or in any case more or less discontinuous ones that enable us now and again to glimpse some fragment of the original subject. This technique is sometimes used by film-makers seeking "honorably" to acquit themselves of tasks they feel unworthy of their talents; some beautiful and relatively "difficult" American films, such as Robert Aldrich's *Kiss Me Deadly*, have resulted. It is Jean-Luc Godard, however, who thus far has derived the most rewarding results from this principle, especially in *Pierrot le fou*. He too starts with a conventional detective story and then proceeds to "cloud the issue" with an extraordinary freedom. A number of events occur in *Pierrot le fou* that are absolutely incomprehensible if the viewer relies only on the deliberately confusing "explanations" offered from time to time. Men of letters will of course maintain that the real subject of *Pierrot le fou* is the love of Marianne and Ferdinand, or perhaps something akin to "the grandeurs and miseries of the modern romantic spirit." But, as was said earlier, a subject is primarily a mainspring of the discourse of a film, a driving force, a seed from which a form germinates; and the detective story that was Godard's starting point, the "plot," provides all these things. Love or a philosophy of life, in and of themselves, are only themes, and a *theme* is not the same thing as a *subject* for a film-maker.

Godard needed the subject of "Pierrot le fou" in order to give *form* to his film. As he structured the work, however, the subject practically disappears from sight in the course of its development. And let it be noted that I use the word "practically" deliberately. The original plot line might, of course, have disappeared entirely, as happened to the de Maupassant story that is supposedly the basis of *Masculin-féminin*. In the case of *Pierrot le fou*, the film might thus have been "stripped down" to the nostalgic wanderings of a man of great inner purity and the woman who will lead him to his death. But stripping the film down in this way would also have deprived it of its underpinnings. Godard has a very different view of the original subject from that of his audience, and he insists on revealing that subject from time to time precisely to remind the audience that he knows it more intimately than they do and has deliberately kept it hidden. On the level of communication, of course, this is tantamount to emphasizing the universal relevance of his story, but more significantly, this narrative method creates a dialectical tension between the subject and the discourse, fragments of the subject appearing and then disappearing in accordance with a rhythm that is quite essential to the discontinuous structure of the film. Godard carried this principle even further in *Made in U.S.A.*, but because of the careless way in which the film was made and perhaps more importantly because of a problem of running time,[3] nothing new is added to the dialectic already contained in *Pierrot le fou*.

As the reader will notice, I use the term "discontinuity" in reference to *Pierrot le fou*. Together with *Vivre sa vie* and *Une Femme mariée*, the film is, in fact, part of the great battle Godard is waging to free himself from the traditional narrative forms of cinema that have their source in the unity and continuity of action of the nineteenth-century novel, and it represents a step toward the creation of new narrative forms based on a "collage" of disparate elements as well as on discontinuity of tone, style, and materials. Although *dis-continuity* of this sort has already been mentioned during my discussion of the dialectics of materials, it must now be viewed from the perspective of the film subject. The choice of a subject for *Pierrot le fou*, or more accurately, the decision made with regard to how the subject was to function, was exercised precisely with an eye to the new narrative form that Godard is intent on creating, whereby the subject of a film will function as a hidden pivot around which *discontinuity* will become *structure*. The quest for some way in which to give form to the discontinuity that underlies all of Godard's work is diametrically opposed to the approach of Robbe-Grillet, who has attempted in his first three films to create works with marked unity and even continuity (although in the process he completely reformulated the empirical unity previously obtained in the novel through such common devices as sustained characterization, unity of style, and continuity of narrative action) in his search for an all-encompassing type of unity, one bringing every element of a film, both narrative and plastic, into an intimate, symbiotic relationship resembling that of certain "lyrical" operatic works such as *Pelléas et Mélisande* or *Wozzeck*. As completely different as these two approaches might appear to be, they nevertheless constitute the most fertile ones of any in contemporary cinema.

Midway between the "straight" but hidden subject of the sort found in *Pierrot le fou* and the apparently concealed but actually "irrational" subject of *Marienbad* and *L'Immortelle*, another type of concealed subject can be distinguished, different both in nature and in function from those in *Pierrot le fou* and *Made in U.S.A.* This third type of subject involves what we might call "the psychology of intimation." It is not the characters' external behavior or the nature of the external events determining their acts that is kept hidden, but rather their innermost motives, the principles underlying the rather strange world they inhabit, the factors that Maurice Blanchot calls "the secret center of everything."[4] Both Blanchot's essays and novels are full of rewarding lessons for the contemporary film-maker seeking new subjects more in accord with the needs of the new language just beginning to develop in cinema. To adapt one of Blanchot's narratives to the screen would be a patently absurd enterprise; Blanchot's subjects can function only within a specifically *literary* set of coordinates. But other subjects fulfilling analogous functions can doubtless play comparable roles within a specifically *cinematic* set of coordinates.

How can these subjects be properly defined? Working within a literary context, Blanchot has defined these subjects in an infinitely more subtle and suggestive manner than could be done here,[5] but, nonetheless, a definition of how these subjects might function in cinema is not impossible, and, however simplistic my approach may be, such a definition may prove useful. Generally speaking, concealed subjects of this sort, although they remain almost as invisible as those that certain critics think they detect buried in the labyrinthine images of *Marienbad*, can eventually be apprehended through a process of interpretation, through a "close reading." In contrast to a Robbe-Grillet film, a subject that "really exists" underlies such works. It is usually expressed in metaphors so personal in nature, however, that quite probably the person responsible for them would not or could not express himself in any other way than in absolute metaphors, metaphors that have no independent meaning, that simply refer to a completely inner world that is, in a sense, beyond "comprehension." If the resulting films seem to demand interpretation, interpretation nonetheless is no more necessary with them than it is in the case of a Robbe-Grillet film or novel. Endeavoring to determine this "secret center of everything," even though this center may really exist in the author's mind, it is not necessarily a viable approach to a work and will in fact almost surely cause it to elude us.[6]

For obvious reasons few films thus far have used Blanchot's particular type of subject. There is one film however that represents a remarkable step toward a solution of the problem of the subject. It deals with this problem in a way that is personally more appealing to me than any other previously mentioned, for it seems to have inherent possibilities of developing into something extremely fruitful, representing as it does a kind of synthesis of the approaches embodied in *Marienbad* and *Pierrot le fou* and retaining all the advantages of both. The film is Ingmar Bergman's *Persona*, perhaps the most beautiful work thus far from this director whose work has evolved so extraordinarily over the years.

The "plot" of this film is usually interpreted as hinging on an exchange of personalities, but, even if this reading is correct, even if that is what Bergman principally had in mind, it nonetheless is an obstacle to any real understanding of the film. It may admittedly "explain" a large part (though not all) of the mysterious events that take place in this deliberately difficult work. But, at the same time, such an explanation masks a whole network of extremely complex and contradictory interrelationships that connect all of the events together and provide the film's superstructure. The film's "secret center," whatever it might be (and even if it is one involving the much discussed exchange of personalities), is used by Bergman to give an aesthetic, polysemic coherence to images and events that have many potential meanings both because of their ambiguous nature and because Bergman and Bergman alone possesses the key to the film, a key that is hidden from the beginning and that rightfully remains so. In individual sequences, certainly, it would appear that possible interpretations are constantly being suggested. Many critics would find it very easy—and very tempting—to interpret the sexual aggression in the amazing sequence of the broken glass in Freudian terms. But would such an analysis bring us any nearer to the tangible reality of the scene? Surely, it would be better to *experience* this scene as it develops, to feel the growing sense of apprehension in the interminable waiting, which has such a powerful effect: The longer it lasts, the stranger the characters' gestures appear to be, as this scene, which in the beginning was not at all intense because of the very large space the shot takes in, becomes more and more fraught with tension. And surely it would be better to simply *experience* the pain of the cut that ultimately results, a wound in itself minor and completely ignored by the characters yet that becomes as aggressively shocking as a major mutilation because of the place it occupies in the plastic and dramatic progression of the scene. We have already noted how absurd it was to seek a political explanation for the scenes from the Vietnam war that the sick woman sees on her television set. The horror of the images and the woman's anguish as she sees them must be *lived*. Interpreting them is tantamount to no longer seeing them. There are perhaps readers who will object that Bergman obviously wants his work to be interpreted. Admirers of a Raoul Walsh or a John Ford know that these directors make films they insist should merely be seen and heard, not interpreted (and these films are nonetheless endlessly interpreted by these same fans). Why then should Bergman be denied the right to share the ambition of a Walsh or a Ford—namely, the creation of films that must simply be *experienced?*

The principle underlying Bergman's approach seems most evident when he abruptly introduces elements foreign to the "action." In actual fact, this is only a more satisfying extension of Eisenstein's concept of "attraction by affinities," a technique that often assumed a rather naïvely metaphorical character in the work of the Russian master (and that he abandoned entirely in his maturity). One of the most sophisticated examples of this technique occurs in *The General Line*, where a jet of spraying water expresses the peasants' joy at receiving their new cream separators and at the same time commingles with the actual spurting of the cream from the spout to create a visual metaphor. In Bergman's case the notion of the image-metaphor is much more functionally integrated into the work. It is at once more abstract (in that the metaphors have no specific referent in the film) and more concrete (in that these intrusions involve the actual material confronting the viewer: film, screen, and arclamp); we are aware of this concreteness, moreover, not only because we are shown the film slipping out of the gate, a burnt-out frame, or a film tear, but also because the ultra-rapid, almost subliminal, style of editing Bergman uses in these passages enables us to experience the material made directly as actual celluloid film than would shots of "normal" duration, where we always have the time (and the space) to lose ourselves a little, to forget that what we are seeing is only light and a strip of film. The fluctuations between our sudden awareness that we are watching a *film* and our total or partial lack of awareness of that fact have as much to do with the dialectics of roles and materials previously described as with the Brechtian "distance effect." In this respect, Bergman seems to have successfully achieved another synthesis, combining two tendencies already dealt with here: one toward a greater organic unity attained through the interaction of overlapping and increasingly complex ambiguities, the other toward a structure based on a discontinuity and disparity of elements. The dialectical interplay between the continuous and the discontinuous is an important component in the underlying rhythm of *Persona.*

It is obvious that an exhaustive outline of the modern film subject and its function in the fiction film has not been presented here. There are, moreover, "nonsubject" films (for example, *The Chelsea Girls*) that present problems of an altogether different order. I feel, however, that I have fulfilled, at least in part, the task I set for myself: that of defining the responsibilities that I and other film-makers must resolutely confront. A film subject must no longer depend merely on our passing literary enthusiasms, on our minor day-to-day concerns, or on our notion of what might be of interest to an audience, even one of our own choosing. We are gradually creating a new cinematic language; let us therefore search out subjects that fit its needs. Moreover, this new language has already resulted in the creation of a totally new type of subject, which I shall call "nonfictional" (primarily in order to avoid its being confused with the old-fashioned documentary), one that functions in an altogether different way from the one I have called the "fictional" subject. The final chapter will deal with this new type of subject.

Notes

1. *Cahiers du Cinéma*, no. 195, p. 66.
2. A unity that is immediately undermined dialectically by the use of a style of musical discourse that is discontinuous and disjunctive. Here, too, the similarities between film form, as it is currently developing, and contemporary music are obvious.
3. *Made in U.S.A.* strikes me (or rather struck me in 1967) as an obvious case of an artificially inflated film, lengthened so as to suit the requirements of distribution. Yet as cinema becomes more and more aware of the organization of durations and the over-all composition of a film, concepts that will make totally new demands on a viewer's memory, it will become increasingly apparent that the traditional ninety minutes' running time that may have been perfectly suitable for the condensed novels characteristic of commercial cinema for so many years will no longer be a satisfactory format. Marcel Hanoun's three best films are each about an hour long and his total intransigence in this and every other respect is one of the reasons his films are not better known (as of 1967; *Le Printemps* (1971), a near masterpiece, runs 80 minutes, but then too *L'Hiver* (1968) is clearly inflated to 80 minutes, which would seem to confirm my hypothesis). This tendency toward shorter films would become more general, I believe, if distribution were organized in a more rational manner. There is, of course, another entirely different type of film that tends to be very long (for example, *The*

Chelsea Girls and other underground films), but only the future will tell whether or not this attempt at making film duration congruent with real duration will be fruitful or not.

4. See his Preface to the French edition of Adolfo Bioy-Casares's novel *El Invención de Morel*. Maurice Blanchot is an important French critic and novelist whose work is thus far known only in France. His fictional writings are among the few significant developments that have grown out of Kafka's "absolute metaphors." An examination of his first novel, quite relevant in this context, will be found in Sartre's essay "Aminadab ou du Fantastique consideré comme un language," in *Situations*, vol. I (New York: French and European Publications, 1969).

5. See in particular *L'Espace littéraire* (Paris: Gallimard, 1955).

6. Susan Sontag writes, in *Against Interpretation* (New York: Farrar Strauss and Giroux, 1966), "In most modern instances, interpretation amounts to the philistine refusal to leave the work of art alone. Real art has the capacity to make us nervous. By reducing the work of art to its content and then interpretating *that*, one tames the work of art. Interpretation makes art manageable, conformable."

10

Nonfictional Subjects

From the earliest beginnings of film, in addition to those pioneers for whom film was essentially a lucrative way of entertaining the public, there were others for whom film principally provided a means with which to inform (and perhaps even propagandize) and educate (and perhaps even indoctrinate) a mass audience. For both Marey during the archaic era of cinema and Lumière during its "primitive" period, it was an article of belief that, in the camera, man had at last found an instrument capable of capturing and recording the "real world" and that its essential function, its sacred mission lay therein. In their view the proper function of film would be the promoting of scientific progress, that great ideal of the beginning of the twentieth century; film would change mankind's perception of the world.

When sound was first introduced, during the heyday of the documentary film whose ideal was this celebration of the "real," John Grierson, the English film producer and theoretician, attempted to base a definitive film ethic on the realistic aspect of the concrete film image, the only one that counted to his way of thinking. In his view, film was necessarily *engagé* (to use a term popular only some twenty years later): "The documentary idea after all demands no more than that the affairs of our time shall be brought to the screen

in any fashion which strikes the imagination and is as rich in ob-
served detail as possible. At one level, this vision may be journalistic;
at another, it may rise to poetry and drama. At yet another level its
aesthetic quality lies in the very lucidity of its exposition."[1] This
belief led him to condemn studio shooting of any kind and to declare
that, when a film director dies, he becomes a cameraman.

This bias, shared for some time by a large number of well-intentioned film-makers, indirectly but profoundly affected the evolution
of cinema in two ways. On the one hand, it imbued a very large
number of talented directors, principally those in England and
America but in Italy and France as well, with a deeply felt sense of
social responsibility (which was presumed to be more imperative
for a film-maker than for other artists, owing both to the popular
nature of his "art" and to its "realistic" nature) that frequently distorted the director's approach to the substance out of which film is
created and that emasculated his work. On the other hand, as the
quotation above demonstrates, this Griersonian ethic presupposes
some form of hierarchy within the very sort of nonfictional film
he advocates, a distinction between a film's message and its poetry, to
adopt Grierson's terminology, the naïve simplicity of which is
fairly characteristic of the whole old-style documentary school—
which for every one of the few works of genuine merit it produced,
such as *Man of Aran* and *Coal Face*, produced hundreds of films
that were as sentimental and insipid as *Louisiana Story*, or as luster-
less and pedantic as the bulk of the films produced by the General
Post Office (GPO) unit that Grierson himself directed.

This takes us to the very heart of our subject. We might ask why
the films produced by the GPO should strike a contemporary viewer
as being so lifeless, so fake, so contrived. It is because the notion of
nonfiction in film has changed radically over the last ten years (a development that has also shed some light on the evolution of the fictional film). Ultimately, Grierson's distinction between the content of
film and its form is no different from the views of an Autant-Lara, just
as Walter Ruttman's approach based on these same hierarchies is
exactly the same as that of a von Sternberg. In each instance, regardless of whether the subject or its treatment is given precedence, the
existence of a hierarchy, of a vertical compartmentalization, is precisely what prevents that fusion of form and content that Grierson

believed he was expounding in his writings and his films but that in actual fact only a few purely fictional films such as *The Blue Angel, M,* and *Vampyr* had attained at the time.

I have already attempted to indicate how this fusion is being brought about in the contemporary fiction films, in a more complex manner than Grierson or even Eisenstein could ever have imagined. This complexity has a specific source: Form and content are two concepts that no longer have any meaning; a vastly more organic synthesis is under way today, based on a notion that is the cornerstone of my own present endeavor; and film-makers are increasingly convinced that everything must function on every level, that form is content, and that content can create form. Contemporary nonfictional film subjects often are scarcely different from those of the old-fashioned documentary. What *has* changed, however, is the manner in which these subjects *function* within a cinematic discourse that has become far more Protean through such recent developments as dialectical interaction between different kinds of film material and between the different roles the camera can play, resulting both from technical improvements (lighter cameras and tape recorders) and from a certain expansion in film vocabulary (as, for instance, the recent rehabilitation of the "jump cut," or cut in which no appreciable change in angle or shot size occurs, and certain other kinds of "bad" matches).

We have seen what role fiction subjects play. We might now consider the function of nonfictional subjects, or at least that of the two types most relevant to contemporary needs: the *film essay* and the *ritual film.* Both types can, of course, assume a great variety of forms and may in fact coexist in the same film, a fact that reveals how arbitrary and oversimplified this distinction is. One hopes it may nonetheless prove useful.

For the contemporary observer, the first significant examples of an essay-type film are Georges Franju's short works. Let us therefore examine how *Le Sang des bêtes* and more importantly *Hôtel des Invalides* differ from the hundreds of films with apparently similar subjects. It should be stressed that Franju's films are only *apparently* similar to previous documentaries. What the old-style documentary-makers took as their "subject"—a passive subject by comparison with the "active" fictional subject—Franju takes as a *theme*, and his subject is, in and of itself, a development or rather, an interpretation, of this theme and it thereby becomes "active."

The aim of the old-school documentary film-makers was an absolutely objective rendering of the world they were filming. They sought to make what they filmed beautiful and clear; for them, this sort of reproduction of reality, as judicious to the mind as it was pleasing to the eye and ear, was its own justification. *Le Sang des bêtes* and particularly *Hôtel des Invalides* are no longer documentaries in this objective sense, their entire purpose being to set forth thesis and antithesis through the very texture of the film. These two films of Franju's are *meditations*, and their subjects a *conflict of ideas*. What is even more important, these conflicts give rise to structures.[1] Therein lies the tremendous originality of these two films, which were to cause nonfiction film production to take an entirely new direction. We might now examine how their subjects function.

A subtle but fundamental ambiguity underlies the sumptuous images of *Hôtel des Invalides*; it can be read either as an attack on war, or (on a level that is perhaps less sophisticated but still perfectly cogent and perfectly "natural" to a good many people) as a flag-waving patriotic film (we must remember that it was commissioned and distributed by the French Ministry of the Army!). The pan showing first a collection of medals on the breast of a veteran and then his hideously disfigured face is obviously an ambiguous, "reversible" figure, as is the device of having the words of a patriotic hymn appear on the screen together with gruesome paintings of military carnage; and what could be more ambivalent than the final shot of the film showing the children of the veterans joyfully walking off into the distance under a magnificent stormy sky.

Historically, *Hôtel des Invalides* represented the first use in the documentary film of a formal approach that previously had been exclusively employed in the fiction film. This, however, does not actually turn the documentary into fictional narrative, as always happened in Flaherty's films, with frequently disastrous results: The young visiting couple in Franju's film cannot be regarded as anything more than a mechanical device providing some sort of continuity, as ambiguous as the rest of the film, whereas the handsome youth in *Louisiana Story* is a fictional character, however fiction may be defined.

Hôtel des Invalides admittedly still possesses certain traits that relate it to the conventional fiction film or documentary: a unity of materials,[2] of tone, and of style, as well as considerable spatial and temporal continuity. *Le Sang des bêtes*, however, already contained the beginnings of a disjunct form because of its breaks in tone and material, and, in the two films that were to follow, Franju carried these explorations in discontinuity even further. These two works (his best ones after *Le Sang des bêtes*) are biographical reflections on the lives of *Le Grand Méliès* and *Monsieur et Madame Curie*. Both films employ what at the time was an almost completely unprecedented alternation between scenes performed by actors (recollections or recreated scenes from their lives), iconographic documents of all sorts, and, in *Le Grand Méliès*, clips from Méliès's films. In this film the authenticity provided by "still-lifes" of actual objects and documents from Méliès's life is carried over into the staged scenes by a surprising yet perfectly logical device: Having Méliès's own son play Méliès. This "historical" presence achieves maximum intensity, with "reality" and artifice becoming one and their dialectical relationship "crystallizing," when Méliès's widow appears during the film's last shots playing herself.[3] Of course, many previous "semifictional" films (such as Dieterle's biographies) as well as later documentaries involving some form of iconographic reminiscence[4] (Resnais's *Van Gogh*, for instance) are based on similar subjects. Because these subjects appear, however, in contexts where dialectics (as I have attempted to define them) are employed only on the most banal "articular" level,[5] they result in structures scarcely more complex than a mere linear depiction of the highlights of a life, organized along the lines of a literary biography or an obituary.

It is not surprising that an artist of Franju's stature could not confine himself for long to the short film without risking losing his creative impetus. Unfortunately, however, the magic that is so much a part of his nonfiction work no longer survives in his fiction features. Though Franju the documentary film-maker has had many imitators, his short films remain unique. In my opinion, he is the only cinematographer to have successfully created, from pre-existing material, films that are truly essays, perfect reflections on nonfictional subjects.

In feature-length film, however, a rather curious attempt of this sort has since been undertaken in Italy, one also involving preconceived (as opposed to purely aleatory) material, Francesco Rosi's film *Salvatore Giuliano*. No doubt the film is less reflective and more journalistic, corresponding more to a "profile," the prose equivalent of Franju's poetic meditations. Using as a basis a subject with such vast implications that it raises fundamental questions regarding the entire social and political situation of Italy today, Rosi, in what would seem to be the one inspired moment of his career, constructs a film whose structure derives precisely from the intricate nature of the subject. Viewed as a whole, the film is very much like a hurricane, if I may be allowed this somewhat far-fetched simile: Fragments of sound and fury fly by, sometimes in nonchronological order, often barely comprehensible,[6] and nearly always contradictory on some level or other. These fragments, moreover, seem to whirl round the calm and empty center or eye of the hurricane, with Giuliano himself never present on screen except as a dead body, thus providing an example of how a metaphor can pass intact from the level of subject to that of form, and be fully functional at both levels. At times the sense of the hero's presence somewhere nearby creates absolutely chilling moments of suspense, with Giuliano in a house not far off or close by behind a door; at other moments this element of suspense is almost completely absent, when events occur that have no direct connection with Giuliano personally. This movement constitutes the principal element of tension and release, as well as being one of the number of ways in which the film differs from previous attempts at historical reconstructions. The essential difference, however, may be this: By choosing a political and contemporary subject, then treating it in a much more scrupulously objective manner than is customary, Rosi endows his subject with the ability to engender form. This approach to a subject of this type is of fundamental interest, and, although the film is often quite academic in texture, the material incorporated quite uniform (new camera roles intervening only secondarily, as when Giuliano's mother plays herself), and the narrative development quite linear, these obstacles are easily avoidable today. We must remember that *Giuliano* was made some time ago, in 1961.

It is Godard, starting with *Vivre sa vie*, who has carried these experiments furthest. In order to transcend the normally constraining function of a film subject, he employs two methods, either alternately or simultaneously: He either uses concealed subjects in the manner I have already described or uses nonfictional subjects, which he deals with as a series of reflections on reality as he sees it. Godard quite frequently is an essayist, or more·accurately a polemicist, although of a completely original type—and one perhaps justifiable only within the context of film-making. That the actual ideas expressed in his films are often specious is a fact of less importance than the way in which they are paraded before us; it is this element of intellectual spectacle that is irreplaceable, not the ideas themselves. This might appropriately be called a "cinema of ideas," but his approach is also and principally an aesthetic attitude, in the same sense that Sartre's essay on Baudelaire is a work of art, no matter what one's opinion of the ideas expressed and despite Sartre's own distinction between art and literature.

The first fruits of an endeavor this innovative are often not viable, and, though *Vivre sa vie* is an unqualified success owing to its dialectic of fiction and nonfiction, *Masculin-féminin*, the quite intriguing *Deux or trois choses que je sais d'elle*, and certainly *La Chinoise* are not successful films.[7] Quite probably, they are not successful because they become more and more experimental. Nevertheless they are steps toward a cinema of the kind long ago dreamed of by directors as dissimilar as Jacques Feyder, who hoped to adapt Montaigne's essays to film, and Eisenstein, who wanted to make a film based on Marx's *Capital*: a cinema of pure reflection, where the subject becomes the basis of an intellectual construct, which in turn is capable of engendering the over-all form and even the texture of a film without being denatured or distorted.

As has already been pointed out, Godard has gone a good deal further in this direction than any other cinema *auteur*.[8] Nevertheless, this is the one area in which he has perhaps been surpassed, interestingly enough by directors who are much less well known and who work for television. The two examples that follow were not chosen for any special superiority, but because they are fairly recent and fairly typical. The first of these is Jean-Pierre Lajournade's *Bruno*. By viewing the subject he chose for this strange program alternately from a sociological and political perspective and from a more intimate existential point of view, Lajournade has laid the foundations for a rather cohesive deliberately shifting structure, which tends at times toward a *cinéma-vérité* style (as when the actors, interviewed by real personnel directors, seem no longer to be acting) and at times toward a pronounced and occasionally clumsy stylization (as when the young man wrestles, either alone or in the company of a girl student of his, with the inner torment that has led him to abandon his studies and look for the first job opening available). Sometimes the transition from one style to the other takes the form of abrupt ellipses, and sometimes it is almost imperceptible, as during the hero's encounter with the snobbish girl, where stylization and improvisation mingle in a rather disquieting way (throughout the film, moreover, it is often difficult to determine the exact nature of the relationship between camera and protagonists).

Another possible approach to this sort of subject is illustrated by Danielle Hunebelle[9] and Jacques Krier's television series *Jeux de société*. It is not so much the fact that nonactors are often called upon to play themselves in dramatizations of social problems as the manner in which these programs are structured that is of interest here. Although in certain episodes of the series the narrative is carried forward essentially by staged scenes, ones skillfully intercut with and commented on by interviews involving people directly concerned with the "problem," in the episode entitled "La Mort d'un honnête homme," this procedure is reversed. Here, the dramatic narrative appears only in a very fragmented, allusive form in the acted scenes but is commented on at length by the interviewees, and the shifts in camera-actor relationship characteristic of the series as a whole consequently assume a very perceptible structural role here, the resulting structures deriving very directly from the contradictions inherent in that splendid platitude—the responsibility of the press. Thus even false problems may provide subjects for reflective films and result in aesthetically viable works.

This writer has already mentioned how much he respects André

S. Labarthe's work for the *Cinéastes de notre temps* series. It might simply be noted here that the dialectics of fiction and nonfiction that seem to be characteristic of nearly every one of the great reflective films of the last few years[10] exist in these programs as well, in the form of an alternation between interviews and film clips such as were described in the discussion of the dialectic of materials. I might now discuss that other important type of nonfictional work, which I have called the ritual film. One should admit from the outset, however, that an analysis of this type is very problematical at this juncture, for this sort of cinema is still in its gestation period.

Although the notion of a cinema of ritual has its source in the experimental film of the 1920's, notably in the films of Man Ray and Hans Richter,[11] the concept did not really take hold until the advent of two successive postwar generations of American experimental film-makers. Almost every film made by the California avant-garde (1940–1955: Curtis Harrington, Maya Deren, James Broughton, Sidney Peterson) has ritual aspects. The formal possibilities implicit in such an approach are exploited with unequal results, a particular feature being the use and abuse of the possibilities of spatial disorientation created through editing. It seems to me that it is Kenneth Anger's two most important films, *Fireworks* and *Inauguration of the Pleasure Dome*, that stand out today as the important contributions. *Inauguration of the Pleasure Dome* involves a ritual in every sense of the word, one freely inspired by the sexual and magical practices of a modern sect and performed before Anger's camera by participants who in some cases were actual members of this sect (thereby peripherally introducing a mixture of the authentic and the fictional). The "inauguration" follows a rigorous symbolic ritual that is completely obscure to the profane spectator (the subject of the film therefore being of the concealed type), and this inexorable progression of symbols provides a framework upon which are grafted luxurious extravagances of color (in make-up, sets, costumes, filtered lights), and at the same time a gradual accumulation of careful superpositions transforms perfectly legible images into pure visual texture. Anger might perhaps be reproached for having let the method employed result in a certain tedium, but, if tedium it is, it is a "heavenly tedium," at least to any sensual eye.

The transformation of a ritual sensuality into visual material is even more successfully achieved in the best film of Ron Rice, whose premature death deprived the new American cinema of one of its most authentic talents. This film, *Chumlum*, superficially resembles certain sections of *Inauguration of the Pleasure Dome*, although here the constant use of multiple superimposed images tends to create a plastic space that at times is quite rigorously articulated (according to the principles outlined in the chapter on editing). The greatest originality of the film lies however in the fact that these spatial articulations become part of a continual flow, in which distinct shots no longer exist; *Chumlum* follows an incredibly complicated rite in the midst of which momentarily emerge extremely complex configurations, color combinations so refined as to be without precedent in cinema.

Stan Brakhage's very interesting film, *Blue Moses*, contains both reflective and ritual elements. Ostensibly a dissertation on the "paradox of the actor," interlarded with considerations that are completely esoteric because they have to do with Brakhage's private life, the film is a kind of ritual essay. Involved in these two inextricably intertwined subjects are constant oppositions between the actor (with make-up) and the actor as man (without make-up), between almost completely abstract images of the surrounding countryside obtained through swish-pans and stable shots "inhabited" by the actor, between the actor and his image on the screen, between the spoken word and silence, and so on, making *Blue Moses* one of the most intriguing attempts at creating a complex dialectic to have come thus far from American cinema.

A final word must be said about the great animator Harry Smith and his feature-length *Heaven and Earth Magic*. Only recently has it been possible to see this film in Paris, and it still is very difficult to write about it. But, if ever a rite, in this case the most compulsive imaginable, has resulted in the direct creation of the form and texture of a film, it is in this enchanting and exasperating work, whose plastic effect is similar to that of Max Ernst's collages and whose obsessive themes resemble the labyrinthine puzzles of Raymond Roussel. Even obsessions here become structures, everything becomes structure, endlessly, systematically, exhaustively, all within a single fixed shot into which objects and people are hurled, simultaneously or separately, as if by the distracted hand of a dreaming god.

Perhaps the most striking conclusion to be drawn from these brief reflections on the subject is that, for the contemporary cinematographer, both fictional and nonfictional subjects assume the same function, the engendering of form. In the fiction film of the past, the subject was chosen either for the literary developments it could lead to or for the visual arabesques that could be woven around it. The documentary film of the past also represented a choice between these two alternatives. There were, admittedly, film-makers who undertook to accomplish *both* ends, but they always approached the tasks *separately*, as the quotation from Grierson indicates. The cinematic revolution now in progress is based on what is essentially a very simple idea: that a subject can engender form and that to choose a subject is to make an aesthetic choice. This idea has a childlike simplicity, yet it is inherently one with incalculable consequences: It is what will enable cinema to become what music has been thus far, the art of arts.

Notes

1. *Grierson on Documentary* (New York: Praeger Publishers, 1972).
2. No doubt because they attempted to prove something, to explain something in *Man with a Movie Camera* and *Triumph of the Will*, Dziga Vertov and Leni Riefenstahl remain the two greatest documentary film-makers of the old school.
3. Although the manner in which Franju uses newsreel shots is quite interesting.
4. We might be told that this is precisely what the GPO unit did with the mail-sorters on the night train and the sailors on the North Sea. Yet what makes this method worth while in Franju's case is that it is used dialectically and is accorded a special place in the structural counterpoint of several methods, whereas in the GPO films the monotonous persistence of a single approach makes them linear and dull, at least to a contemporary viewer.
5. Although Dziga Vertov's *Three Songs for Lenin* anticipates Franju's films to some extent.
6. In the sense that any shot change involves the continuity-discontinuity principle.
7. The film might be less obscure to the Italian viewer, although not necessarily.
8. I would certainly not defend this viewpoint in these terms today.
9. Jean Rouch's ethnographic and sociological films are obviously reflections of

a kind, but I have already discussed his work and do not feel that examining the manner in which the subject functions in his films would contribute substantially to this chapter.

10. Danielle Hunebelle has since produced for American television "Blacks for Neighbors."

11. As indicated in the Preface, this hasty tribute to the new American cinema dates from a period when I was neither familiar with nor very sympathetic toward the bulk of its major achievements. And, though the concept of a ritual cinema may still be a seminal one with regard to the work of Anger, I should not deal with Hans Richter in these terms today, when I am primarily concerned with the problems of perception training and a scientific exploration of the medium.

Index